Breathes there the man, with soul so dead,
Who never to himself hath said,
*   This is my own, my native land!. . .*
The wretch, concentred all in self,
Living, shall forfeit fair renown,
And, doubly dying, shall go down
To the vile dust, from whence he sprung,
Unwept, unhonour'd, and unsung.

SIR WALTER SCOTT

Breathes

Heroic Ballads & Poems

La Salle, Illinois

There the Man

of the English-Speaking Peoples

Edited by FRANK S. MEYER

Open Court ❄ 1973

ACKNOWLEDGMENTS

The editor gratefully acknowledges permission to reproduce copyright poems in this book.

Stephen Vincent Benet: Invocation from *John Brown's Body*. Published by Holt, Rinehart and Winston, Inc. Copyright, 1927, 1928 by Stephen Vincent Benet; copyright renewed, 1955, 1956 by Rosemary Carr Benet. Reprinted by permission of Brandt & Brandt.

Rupert Brooke: "Peace" and "The Soldier." Reprinted by permission of Dodd, Mead & Company, Inc. from *The Collected Poems of Rupert Brooke*. Copyright 1915 by Dodd, Mead & Company; copyright renewed 1943 by Edward Marsh.

G. K. Chesterton: "Lepanto." Reprinted by permission of Dodd, Mead & Company, Inc. from *The Collected Poems of G. K. Chesterton*. Copyright 1932 by Dodd, Mead & Company, Inc.; Copyright renewed.

A. E. Housman: "Epitaph on an Army of Mercenaries" and "The Oracles." From *The Collected Poems of A. E. Housman*. Copyright 1922 by Holt, Rinehart and Winston, Inc. Copyright 1950 by Barclays Bank Limited. Reprinted by permission of Holt, Rinehart and Winston, Inc.

John McCrae: "In Flanders Fields." Reprinted by permission of G. P. Putnam's Sons from *In Flanders Fields and Other Poems*, by John McCrae. Copyright 1919, 1946, by G. P. Putnam's Sons.

Alan Seeger: "I Have A Rendezvous with Death." Reprinted by permission of Charles Scribner's Sons from *Poems* by Alan Seeger. Copyright 1916 Charles Scribner's Sons; renewal copyright 1944 Elsie Adams Seeger.

Printed in the United States of America

ISBN: 0-87548-143-4

Library of Congress Catolog Card Number: 73-82784

TO THE

AMERICAN SOLDIERS

WHO FELL IN INDOCHINA

CONTENTS

N.B.—*Dates, where appended to the titles of poems,
are those of the events described.*

INTRODUCTION

THE PURPOSE OF THIS BOOK is to fill a gap created by the aesthetic prejudices of these times—to bring together in a single volume outstanding examples of heroic and patriotic poetry in the English language. As a lover of such verse, I have searched high and low and found no such collection published in the past fifty years.

As heroism and patriotism have gone out of fashion, so, or even more so, has the poetry based upon heroic and patriotic themes been neglected over the past decades. Furthermore, since most of the received poetry of the century has been difficult, abstruse, and more or less obscure, the makers of heroic and patriotic verse have been condemned as mere writers of jingles. While it may be admitted that there is little in this genre that will stand with the very greatest poetry, there is a great deal that is excellent. As I hope this book will prove, the writers of such verse have created much that will stand on its own merits—subject apart.

The current objections to matter and to style are indeed closely interconnected. As T. S. Eliot has written in his defense of the verse of Rudyard Kipling: "The starting point for Kipling's verse is the motive of the ballad-maker; and the modern ballad is a type of verse for the appreciation of which we are not provided with the proper critical tools. We are therefore inclined to dismiss the poems, by reference to poetic criteria which do not apply."

That is what these poems are, in spirit if not always technically —ballads. They are ballads in the great tradition, not the complaints that characterize so many contemporary songs that represent the decay of the ballad tradition; but affirmations of the nobility of the human spirit, of courage and devotion. It is by their achievement of a proper expression of such sentiments that they must be judged.

I do not say that all that is included in this book is authentic poetry; some of it is merely rousing verse. But all of it celebrates the lofty in man.

Let it, however, speak for itself. I have but one suggestion for the readers of this book. Read these poems aloud. They are made, like the poetry of the Ancients, to be spoken, not read on the silent page. They will, I predict, make the blood run and the heart beat faster.

FRANK S. MEYER

Although Frank had this anthology in mind for many years, its accomplishment was greatly assisted through his association with Jared Lobdell. Early in their acquaintance they discovered their mutual love of heroic and patriotic verse and chanted, say, stanzas of "Lepanto," "*The Revenge*," or "Horatius" at each other across the dinner table or during the long nights of conversation at Woodstock. With Jared's active assistance in suggesting poems and securing copies of those not in Frank's library, the manuscript grew and was ready for publication before Frank's death in April 1972. I acknowledge for Frank his grateful appreciation of Jared's stimulating and indispensable assistance.

MRS. FRANK S. MEYER

AMERICA

THE WAR OF INDEPENDENCE

The Boston Tea Tax [1773]

ANONYMOUS

I snum I am a Yankee lad, and I guess I'll sing a ditty,
And if you do not relish it the more 'twill be the pity.
    That is, I think I should have been
    A plaguey sight more finished man,
If I'd been born in Boston Town, but I warn't cause I'm a countryman!
    Tol-le-lol-de-riddle, Tol-le-lol-de-ray...

And t'other day the Yankee folks were mad about the taxes,
And so we went like Injuns dressed to split tea chests with axes;
    It was the year of seventy-three
    And we felt really gritty.
The Mayor he would have led the gang, but Boston ain't a city!
    Tol-le-lol-de-riddle, Tol-le-lol-de-ray...

And then aboard the ships we went our vengeance to administer,
And we didn't care one tarnal bit for any king or minister.
    We made a plaguey mess of tea
    In one of the biggest dishes,
I mean we steeped it in the sea and treated all the fishes.
    Tol-le-lol-de-riddle, Tol-le-lol-de-ray...

Free America [1774]

JOSEPH WARREN

That seat of Science, Athens,
And earth's proud mistress, Rome;
Where now are all their glories?
We scarce can find a tomb.
Then guard your rights, Americans.
Nor stoop to lawless sway;
Oppose, oppose, oppose, oppose,
    For North America.

We led fair Freedom hither,
And lo, the desert smiled!
A paradise of pleasure
Was opened in the wild!
Your harvest, bold Americans,
No power shall snatch away!
Huzza, huzza, huzza, huzza,
    For free America.

Torn from a world of tyrants,
Beneath this western sky,
We formed a new dominion,
A land of liberty:
The world shall own we're masters here;
Then hasten on the day:
Huzza, huzza, huzza, huzza,
    For free America.

Proud Albion bowed to Caesar,
And numerous lords before;
To Picts, to Danes, to Normans,
And many masters more:
But we can boast, Americans,
We've never fallen a prey;
Huzza, huzza, huzza, huzza,
    For free America.

God bless this maiden climate,
And through its vast domain
May hosts of heroes cluster,
Who scorn to wear a chain:
And blast the venal sycophant
That dares our rights betray;
Huzza, huzza, huzza, huzza,
    For free America.

Lift up your hands, ye heroes,
And swear with proud disdain,
The wretch that would ensnare you,
Shall lay his snares in vain:
Should Europe empty all her force,
We'll meet her in array,
And fight and shout, and shout and fight
    For North America.

Some future day shall crown us,
The masters of the main,
Our fleets shall speak in thunder
To England, France, and Spain;
And the nations over the ocean spread
Shall tremble and obey
The sons, the sons, the sons, the sons
    Of brave America.

Paul Revere's Ride [1775]

HENRY WADSWORTH LONGFELLOW

Listen, my children, and you shall hear
Of the midnight ride of Paul Revere,
On the eighteenth of April, in Seventy-five;
Hardly a man is now alive
Who remembers that famous day and year.

He said to his friend, "If the British march
By land or sea from the town tonight,
Hang a lantern aloft in the belfry arch
Of the North Church tower as a signal light,—
One, if by land, and two, if by sea;
And I on the opposite shore will be,
Ready to ride and spread the alarm
Through every Middlesex village and farm,
For the country-folk to be up and to arm."

Then he said, "Good night!" and with muffled oar
Silently rowed to the Charlestown shore,
Just as the moon rose over the bay,
Where swinging wide at her moorings lay
The Somerset, British man-of-war;
A phantom ship, with each mast and spar
Across the moon like a prison bar,
And a huge black hulk that was magnified
By its own reflection in the tide.

Meanwhile, his friend, through alley and street,
Wanders and watches with eager ears,
Till in the silence around him he hears
The muster of men at the barrack door,
The sound of arms, and the tramp of feet,
And the measured tread of the grenadiers,
Marching down to their boats on the shore.

Then he climbed to the tower of the church,
Up the wooden stairs, with stealthy tread,
To the belfry-chamber overhead,
And startled the pigeons from their perch
On the sombre rafters, that round him made

Masses and moving shapes of shade,—
Up the trembling ladder, steep and tall,
To the highest window in the wall,
Where he paused to listen and look down
A moment on the roofs of the town,
And the moonlight flowing over all.

Beneath, in the churchyard, lay the dead,
In their night-encampment on the hill,
Wrapped in silence so deep and still
That he could hear, like a sentinel's tread,
The watchful night-wind, as it went
Creeping along from tent to tent,
And seeming to whisper, "All is well!"
A moment only he feels the spell
Of the place and the hour, and the secret dread
Of the lonely belfry and the dead;
For suddenly all his thoughts are bent
On a shadowy something far away,
Where the river widens to meet the bay,—
A line of black that bends and floats
On the rising tide, like a bridge of boats.

Meanwhile, impatient to mount and ride,
Booted and spurred, with a heavy stride
On the opposite shore walked Paul Revere.
Now he patted his horse's side,
Now gazed at the landscape far and near,
Then, impetuous, stamped the earth,
And turned and tightened his saddle-girth;
But mostly he watched with eager search
The belfry-tower of the Old North Church,
As it rose above the graves on the hill,
Lonely and spectral and sombre and still.
And lo! as he looks, on the belfry's height
A glimmer, and then a gleam of light!
He springs to the saddle, the bridle he turns,
But lingers and gazes, till full on his sight
A second lamp in the belfry burns!

A hurry of hoofs in a village street,
A shape in the moonlight, a bulk in the dark,
And beneath, from the pebbles, in passing, a spark
Struck out by a steed flying fearless and fleet;

That was all! And yet, through the gloom and the light,
The fate of a nation was riding that night;
And the spark struck out by that steed, in his flight,
Kindled the land into flame with its heat.

He has left the village and mounted the steep,
And beneath him, tranquil and broad and deep,
Is the Mystic, meeting the ocean tides;
And under the alders, that skirt its edge,
Now soft on the sand, now loud on the ledge,
Is heard the tramp of his steed as he rides.

It was twelve by the village clock
When he crossed the bridge into Medford town.
He heard the crowing of the cock,
And the barking of the farmer's dog,
And felt the damp of the river fog,
That rises after the sun goes down.

It was one by the village clock,
When he galloped into Lexington.
He saw the gilded weathercock
Swim in the moonlight as he passed,
And the meeting-house windows blank and bare,
Gaze at him with a spectral glare,
As if they already stood aghast
At the bloody work they would look upon.

It was two by the village clock,
When he came to the bridge in Concord town.
He heard the bleating of the flock,
And the twitter of birds among the trees,
And felt the breath of the morning breeze
Blowing over the meadows brown.
And one was safe and asleep in his bed
Who at the bridge would be first to fall,
Who that day would be lying dead,
Pierced by a British musket-ball.

You know the rest. In the books you have read,
How the British Regulars fired and fled,—
How the farmers gave them ball for ball,
From behind each fence and farmyard wall,
Chasing the red-coats down the lane,
Then crossing the fields to emerge again
Under the trees at the turn of the road,
And only pausing to fire and load.

So through the night rode Paul Revere;
And so through the night went his cry of alarm
To every Middlesex village and farm,—
A cry of defiance and not of fear,
A voice in the darkness, a knock at the door,
And a word that shall echo forevermore!
For, borne on the night-wind of the Past,
Through all our history, to the last,
In the hour of darkness and peril and need,
The people will waken and listen to hear
The hurrying hoof-beats of that steed,
And the midnight message of Paul Revere.

Concord Hymn [1775]

RALPH WALDO EMERSON

By the rude bridge that arched the flood,
   Their flag to April's breeze unfurled,
Here once the embattled farmers stood,
   And fired the shot heard round the world.

The foe long since in silence slept;
   Alike the conqueror silent sleeps;
And Time the ruined bridge has swept
   Down the dark stream which seaward creeps.

On the green bank, by this soft stream,
   We set to-day a votive stone;
That memory may their dead redeem,
   When, like our sires, our sons are gone.

Spirit, that made those heroes dare
   To die, and leave their children free,
Bid Time and Nature gently spare
   The shaft we raise to them and thee.

The Ballad of Bunker Hill [1775]

ANONYMOUS

The soldiers from town to the foot of the hill,
In barges and rowboats, some great and some small,
They pottered and dawdled and twaddled until
We feared there would be no attack after all.

>Let the foeman draw nigh till the white of his eye
>Comes in range with your rifles, and then let it fly,
>And show to Columbia, to Britain and fame,
>How justice smiles aweful when freemen take aim!

But when they got ready and all came along,
The way they marched up the hillside wasn't slow;
We were not a-feared and we welcomed 'em strong,
Held fire till the word and then laid the lads low.

>But who shall declare the end of the affair,
>At sundown there wasn't a man of us there;
>We didn't depart till we'd given 'em some,
>We used up our powder and had to go home!

Warren's Address [1775]

JOHN PIERPONT

Stand! the ground's your own, my braves!
Will ye give it up to slaves?
Will ye look for greener graves?
    Hope ye mercy still?
What's the mercy despots feel?
Hear it in that battle-peal!
Read it on yon bristling steel!
    Ask it,—ye who will.

Fear ye foes who kill for hire?
Will ye to your homes retire?
Look behind you!—they're a-fire!
    And, before you, see
Who have done it! From the vale
On they come!—and will ye quail?
Leaden rain and iron hail
    Let their welcome be!

In the God of battles trust;
Die we may,—and die we must;
But, oh, where can dust to dust
    Be consign'd so well,
As where Heaven its dews shall shed
On the martyr'd patriot's bed,
And the rocks shall raise their head
    Of his deeds to tell?

The Death of Warren [1775]

ANONYMOUS

When the war-cry of Liberty rang through the land,
We sprang to our arms the foe to withstand;
On old Bunker Hill their entrenchments they rear
When the army is joined by a young volunteer.
Tempt not death, cried his friends, but he bade them good-bye,
Saying, Oh, it is sweet for my country to die!

The tempest of battle now rages and swells,
Mid the thunder of cannon and pealing of bells;
A light, not of battle, illumines yon spire—
Scene of woe and destruction, 'tis Charlestown on fire.
The young volunteer heedeth not the sad cry
But murmurs, 'tis sweet for my country to die!

Now our powder is spent and they rally again,
Retreat, says our chief, since unarmed we remain,
But the young volunteer lingers yet on the field,
Reluctant to fly and disdaining to yield.
A shot!—Ah, he falls—but his life's latest sigh,
'Tis sweet, oh, 'tis sweet for my country to die!

WILLIAM ROSS WALLACE

He lay upon his dying bed;
　　His eye was growing dim,
When with a feeble voice he called
　　His weeping son to him:
"Weep not, my boy!" the vet'ran said,
　　"I bow to Heaven's high will,—
But quickly from yon antlers bring
　　The sword of Bunker Hill."

The sword was brought, the soldier's eye
　　Lit with a sudden flame;
And as he grasp'd the ancient blade,
　　He murmured Warren's name:
Then said, "My boy, I leave you gold,—
　　But what is richer still,
I leave you, mark me, mark me now—
　　The sword of Bunker Hill.

"'Twas on that dread, immortal day,
　　I dared the Briton's band,
A Captain raised this blade on me—
　　I tore it from his hand;
And while the glorious battle raged,
　　It lightened freedom's will—
For, boy, the God of freedom blessed
　　The sword of Bunker Hill.

"Oh, keep the sword!"—his accents broke—
　　A smile—and he was dead—
But his wrinkled hand still grasped the blade
　　Upon that dying bed.
The son remains; the sword remains—
　　Its glory growing still—
And twenty millions bless the sire,
　　And sword of Bunker Hill.

The Bombardment of Bristol, R.I. [1775]

ANONYMOUS

In seventeen hundred seventy-five,
Our Bristol town was much surprised
By a thievish pack of villains
Who will not work to earn their livings.

October, 'twas the seventh day,
As I have heard the people say,
Wallace—his name be ever curst,
Came on our harbour just at dusk.

And there his ship did safely moor
And quickly sent his barge ashore,
With orders that should not be broke,
Or that we might expect a smoke.

Demanding that our magistrates
Should quickly come on board his ship
And let him have some sheep and cattle
Or that they might expect a battle.

At eight o'clock by signal given,
Our peaceful atmosphere was riven;
Women with children in their arms
With doleful cries ran to the farms.

With all their firing and their skill
They did not any person kill,
Neither was any person hurt
Except the Reverend Parson Burt.

And he was not killed by a ball,
As judged by jurors one and all,
But being in a sickly state,
He frightened fell, which proved his fate.

Another truth to you I'll tell
That you may see they levelled well,
For aiming for to kill the people,
They fired their shot into a steeple.

They fired low, they fired high,
The women scream, the children cry,
And all their firing and their racket
Shot off the topmast of a packet!

Liberty Tree [1775]

THOMAS PAINE

In a chariot of light from the regions of day,
    The Goddess of Liberty came;
Ten thousand celestials directed the way
    And hither conducted the dame.
A fair budding branch from the gardens above,
    Where millions with millions agree,
She brought in her hand as a pledge of her love,
    And the plant she named *Liberty Tree*.

The celestial exotic struck deep in the ground,
    Like a native it flourished and bore;
The fame of its fruit drew the nations around,
    To seek out this peaceable shore.
Unmindful of names or distinction they came,
    For freemen like brothers agree;
With one spirit enbued, they one friendship pursued.
    And their temple was *Liberty Tree*.

Beneath this fair tree, like the patriarchs of old,
    Their bread in contentment they ate,
Unvexed with the troubles of silver and gold.
    The cares of the grand and the great.
With timber and tar they Old England supplied,
    And supported her power on the sea;
Her battles they fought, without getting a groat,
    For the honor of *Liberty Tree*.

But hear, O ye swains, 'tis a tale most profane,
    How all the tyrannical powers,
Kings, Commons, and Lords, are uniting amain,
    To cut down this guardian of ours;
From the east to the west blow the trumpet to arms
    Through the land let the sound of it flee,
Let the far and the near, all unite with a cheer,
    In defence of our *Liberty Tree*.

Nathan Hale [1776]

FRANCIS MILES FINCH

To drum-beat and heart-beat a soldier marches by,
There is color in his cheek, there is courage in his eye;
To drum-beat and heart-beat in a moment he must die.
    By the starlight and moonlight he seeks the Briton's camp,
    He hears the rustling flag and the armed sentry's tramp;
And the starlight and moonlight his silent wand'rings lamp.

A sharp clang—a steel clang, and terror in the sound!
For the sentry falcon-eyed, in the camp a spy has found;
A sharp clang—a steel clang, the patriot is bound.
    Neath the blue morn, the sunny morn, he dies upon the tree;
    He mourns that he can lose but one life for Liberty;
In the blue morn, the sunny morn, his spirit wings are free!

Nathan Hale [1776]

ANONYMOUS

The breezes went steadily thro' the tall pines,
  A-saying "oh! hu-ush!" a-saying "oh! hu-ush!"
As stilly stole by a bold legion of horse,
  For Hale in the bush; for Hale in the bush.

"Keep still!" said the thrush as she nestled her young,
  In a nest by the road; in a nest by the road.
"For the tyrants are near, and with them appear,
  What bodes us no good; what bodes us no good."

The brave captain heard it, and thought of his home,
  In a cot by the brook; in a cot by the brook.
With mother and sister and memories dear,
  He so gaily forsook; he so gaily forsook.

Cooling shades of the night were coming apace,
  The tattoo had beat; the tattoo had beat.
The noble one sprang from his dark lurking place,
  To make his retreat; to make his retreat.

He warily trod on the dry rustling leaves,
  As he pass'd thro' the wood; as he pass'd thro' the wood;
And silently gained his rude launch on the shore,
  As she play'd with the flood; as she play'd with the flood.

The guards of the camp, on that dark, dreary night,
  Had a murderous will; had a murderous will.
They took him and bore him afar from the shore,
  To a hut on the hill; to a hut on the hill.

No mother was there, nor a friend who could cheer,
  In that little stone cell; in that little stone cell.
But he trusted in love, from his father above.
  In his heart all was well; in his heart all was well.

An ominous owl with his solemn base voice,
  Sat moaning hard by; sat moaning hard by.
"The tyrant's proud minions most gladly rejoice,
  For he must soon die; for he must soon die."

The brave fellow told them, no thing he restrain'd,
    The cruel gen'ral; the cruel gen'ral.
His errand from camp, of the ends to be gain'd,
    And said that was all; and said that was all.

They took him and bound him and bore him away,
    Down the hill's grassy side; down the hill's grassy side.
'Twas there the base hirelings, in royal array,
    His cause did deride; his cause did deride.

Five minutes were given, short moments, no more,
    For him to repent; for him to repent;
He pray'd for his mother, he ask'd not another,
    To Heaven he went; to Heaven he went.

The faith of a martyr, the tragedy shew'd,
    As he trod the last stage; as he trod the last stage.
And Britons will shudder at gallant Hale's blood,
    As his words do presage, as his words do presage.

"Thou pale king of terrors, thou life's gloomy foe,
    Go frighten the slave, go frighten the slave;
Tell tyrants, to you, their allegiance they owe.
    No fears for the brave; no fears for the brave."

Yankee Doodle

RICHARD SHUCKBURG

Father and I went down to camp,
　　Along with Cap'n Goodin',
And there we saw the men and boys
　　As thick as hasty pudding.

　　Yankee Doodle, keep it up,
　　　Yankee Doodle dandy,
　　Mind the music and the step,
　　　And with the girls be handy.

And there we see a thousand men,
　　As rich as Squire David;
And what they wasted ev'ry day,
　　I wish it could be saved.

The 'lasses they eat ev'ry day,
　　Would keep a house a winter;
They have so much that, I'll be bound,
　　They eat it when they've mind ter.

And there I see a swamping gun,
　　Large as a log of maple,
Upon a deuced little cart,
　　A load for father's cattle.

And every time they shoot it off,
　　It takes a horn of powder,
And makes a noise like father's gun,
　　Only a nation louder.

I went as nigh to one myself
　　As 'Siah's underpinning;
And father went as nigh agin,
　　I thought the deuce was in him.

Cousin Simon grew so bold,
　　I thought he would have cocked it;
It scared me so I shrinked it off
　　And hung by father's pocket.

And Cap'n Davis had a gun,
　　He kind of clapt his hand on 't,
And stuck a crooked stabbing iron
　　Upon the little end on 't.

And there I see a pumpkin shell
　　As big as mother's basin;
And every time they touched it off
　　They scampered like the nation.

I see a little barrel too,
　　The heads were made of leather;
They knocked upon 't with little clubs
　　And called the folks together.

And there was Cap'n Washington,
　　And gentlefolks about him;
They say he's grown so 'tarnal proud,
　　He will not ride without 'em.

He got him on his meeting clothes
　　Upon a slapping stallion,
He set the world along in rows,
　　In hundreds and in millions.

The flaming ribbons in his hat,
　　They looked so taring fine, ah,
I wanted dreadfully to get
　　To give to my Jemima.

I see another snarl of men
　　A-digging graves, they told me,
So 'tarnal long, so 'tarnal deep,
　　They 'tended they should hold me.

It scared me so I hooked it off,
　　Nor stopped, as I remember,
Nor turned about till I got home,
　　Locked up in mother's chamber.

The Maryland Battalion [1776]

JOHN W. PALMER

Spruce Macaronis, and pretty to see,
Tidy and dapper and gallant were we;
Blooded, fine gentlemen, proper and tall,
Bold in a fox-hunt and gay at a ball;
Prancing soldados so martial and bluff,
Billets for bullets, in scarlet and buff,—
But our cockades were clasped with a mother's low prayer,
And the sweethearts that braided the sword-knots were fair.

There was grummer of drums humming hoarse in the hills,
And the bugle sang fanfaron down by the mills;
By Flatbush the bagpipes were droning amain,
And keen cracked the rifles in Martense's lane;
For the Hessians were flecking the hedges with red,
And the grenadiers' tramp marked the roll of the dead.

Three to one, flank and rear, flashed the files of St. George,
The fierce gleam of their steel as the glow of a forge.
The brutal boom-boom of their swart cannoneers
Was sweet music compared with the taunt of their cheers—
For the brunt of their onset, our crippled array,
And the light of God's leading gone out in the fray!

Oh, the rout on the left and the tug on the right!
The mad plunge of the charge and the wreck of the flight!
When the cohorts of Grant held stout Stirling at strain,
And the mongrels of Hesse went tearing the slain;
When at Freeke's Mill the flumes and the sluices ran red,
And the dead choked the dyke and the marsh choked the dead!

"O Stirling, good Stirling! how long must we wait?
Shall the shout of your trumpet unleash us too late?
Have you never a dash for brave Mordecai Gist,
With his heart in his throat, and his blade in his fist?
Are we good for no more than to prance in a ball,
When the drums beat the charge and the clarions call?"

Tralara! Tralara! Now praise we the Lord
For the clang of His call and the flash of His sword!
Tralara! Tralara! Now forward to die;
For the banner, hurrah! and for sweethearts, good-bye!
"Four hundred wild lads!" Maybe so. I'll be bound
'Twill be easy to count us, face up, on the ground.
If we hold the road open tho' Death take the toll,
We'll be missed on parade when the States call the roll—
When the flags meet in peace and the guns are at rest,
And fair Freedom is singing Sweet Home in the West.

Riflemen's Song at Bennington |1777|

ANONYMOUS

Why come ye hither, Redcoats, your mind what madness fills?
In our valleys there is danger, and there's danger on our hills!
Oh hear ye not the singing of the bugle wild and free?
Full soon ye'll know the ringing of the rifle from the tree!
For the rifle—the rifle, in our hands will prove no trifle!

Ye ride a goodly steed; ye may know another master;
Ye forward come with speed, but ye'll learn to back much faster.
When ye meet our mountain boys and their leader Johnny Stark,
Lads who make but little noise, lads who always hit the mark!
For the rifle—the rifle, in our hands will prove no trifle!

Had ye no graves at home across the briny water
That hither ye must come like bullocks to the slaughter?
If we the work must do, why the sooner 'tis begun.
If flint and trigger hold but true, the quicker 'twill be done!
For the rifle—the rifle, in our hands will prove no trifle!

The Yankee Man-of-War

ANONYMOUS

'Tis of a gallant Yankee ship that flew the stripes and stars,
And the whistling wind from the west-nor'-west blew through the pitch-pine spars;
With her starboard tacks aboard, my boys, she hung upon the gale;
On an autumn night we raised the light on the old Head of Kinsale.

It was a clear and cloudless night, and the wind blew steady and strong,
As gayly over the sparkling deep our good ship bowled along;
With the foaming seas beneath her bow the fiery waves she spread,
And bending low her bosom of snow, she buried her lee cat-head.

There was no talk of short'ning sail by him who walked the poop,
And under the press of her pond'ring jib, the boom bent like a hoop!
And the groaning water-ways told the strain that held her stout main-tack,
But he only laughed as he glanced aloft at a white and silvery track.

The mid-tide meets in the Channel waves that flow from shore to shore,
And the mist hung heavy upon the land from Featherstone to Dunmore,
And that sterling light in Tusker Rock where the old bell tolls each hour,
And the beacon light that shone so bright was quench'd on Waterford Tower.

The nightly robes our good ship wore were her whole topsails three,
Her spanker and her standing jib—the courses being free,
"Now, lay aloft! my heroes bold, not a moment must be passed!"
And royals and top-gallant sails were quickly on each mast.

What looms upon our starboard bow? What hangs upon the breeze?
'Tis time our good ship hauled her wind abreast the old Saltees,
For by her ponderous press of sail and by her consorts four
We saw our morning visitor was a British man-of-war.

Up spake our noble Captain then, as a shot ahead of us past—
"Haul snug your flowing courses! lay your topsail to the mast!"
Those Englishmen gave three loud hurrahs from the deck of their covered ark,
And we answered back by a solid broadside from the decks of our patriot bark.

"Out booms! out booms!" our skipper cried, "out booms and give her sheet,"
And the swiftest keel that was ever launched shot ahead of the British fleet,
And amidst a thundering shower of shot, with stun'-sails hoisting away,
Down the North Channel Paul Jones did steer just at the break of day.

The Ballad of Benjamin Bones [1779]

CHRISTOPHER WARD

Oh my name it is Benjamin Bones
    And I remembers well
How I took a trip on a fightin' ship
    Of which you have heard tell.
Bon Homme Richard they calls her name.
    Her cap'n was John Paul Jones.
She carried a crew of a hundred and two,
    And her bos'n was Benjamin Bones.

We'd sailed nor'east and we'd sailed nor'west
    For a week or two or three,
When the topmast-boy yells, "Deck ahoy!
    A distant sail I see."
I took a squint at her, nigh hull down,
    And says, "That ship, by gee,
By her size and her shape is the brig Serapis,
    And she's twicet as big as we"—

Says the cap'n, "Well, Bones, I ask ye now,
    Shall we fight her or give her the slip?"
"I'm a son-of-a-gun," says I, "if I'll run
    From a blasted British ship
No matter if she's bigger than us
    By a couple of thousand tons;
It ain't the size that takes the prize.
    It's the men behind the guns!"
Then he looks at me and I looks at him,
    My eye was as cold as ice.
So he says, "I'll try, if you'll stand by
    And gimme your best advice."
"Then damn the torpedoes and go ahead!"
    I says to Captain Jones.
For you can depend to the very end
    On Bos'n Benjamin Bones.

So he sends the jollies all aloft
    To shake out every rag,
And, when we comes near to old beef-and-beer,
    We histes our battle flag,

"Ye may fire when ready, Jones," I said.
  "Thar lies the old Serape.
And, if I was you, I know what I'd do.
  I'd give her a whiff of grape
And double shot the guns," I says.
  "And double charge 'em, too.
And a double grog would give *us* a jog
  For what *we* got to do."
Then he gives the orders like I says
  And we had our fill of rum.
So we gives three cheers, while the cannoneers
  Gives the enemy kingdom-come!

The cannons roared and the muskets cracked
  And the cannons roared again.
And the balls comes a-thumpin' and bouncin' and bumpin'
  And knockin' over our men.
And one of 'em hits our mizzen-mast
  And cuts it away to a stump.
Then the mainmast was gashed so bad that it crashed,
  And that gives our captain the hump.
"Oh, Bos'n Bones," the captain says,
  "They've sure got us fair on the hip."
But I makes reply, "Don't never say die!
  And don't never give up the ship!"
Then overboard the foremast goes,
  And the rudder gets shot away.
Says Captain Jones, "Oh, Bos'n Bones,
  Now what have ye got to say?
We ain't got no mast, nor rudder, nor sails
  And hardly any men.
Please be precise with your advice,
  I'm leanin' on ye, Ben!"

Just then there comes an awful roar,
  A regular hullabaloo.
All the guns, double loaded, had gone and exploded
  And killed all the rest of the crew.
And they'd blowed the bottom right out of the ship
  And she was a-sinkin' fast.

Then I says to him, "Well, douse my glim!
    This looks like trouble at last.
But the Old Guard never surrenders," I says.
    "No matter how bad the scrape.
If this here boat won't stay afloat,
    We'll board the old Serape!
Come on," says I, as I climbs aboard
    The enemy lyin' by,
While the crew all stares and the captain glares
    Through the monickle in his eye.

"Disperse, ye rebels! Lay down yer arms!"
    Says he, in angry tones,
Says I, "Think twice before givin' advice
    To Bos'n Benjamin Bones."
"You're twicet as big as me," I says,
    "But I won't take none of your lip.
Come on, you limey!" I says. "Gor blimey,
    I'll fight ye for yer ship!
If ye got any sportin' blood in yer veins,
    Come on and fight, my beauty!
For old George Rex and all England expec's
    Every man to do his duty!"
At that all his crew gives a lusty cheer
    On seein' their captain defied.
And then, by jing, they forms a ring
    With me and the captain inside!

He puts up his dukes and makes a pass,
    But I ducks and lands on his map.
Says he, "By Jove! You're a stalwart cove.
    That there was a nahsty rap!"
"You ain't seen nothin' yet," I says.
    "I ain't begun to fight!"
Then I squares off at that bloomin' toff
    And lets him have my right.
It takes him fair on the point of his chin
    And knocks him heels over head,
He hits the deck with the back of his neck
    And lays there like he's dead.
And one of his eyes was black as ink
    And t'other was indigo blue
And his face was a joke, for his jaw was broke
    And his features was all askew.

"Kiss me, Hardy!" was all he said,
    Whatever that may mean.
So his mate counts him out and his crew gives a shout
    To welcome the new champeen.

Then I makes 'em haul down their old red rag
    And histe the Stripes and Stars,
Which our new recruits at once salutes,
    While we serves out rum and cigars.
"We've met the enemy and they're ours!"
    I says to Captain Jones.
"So take this ship on her homeward trip."
    Says he, "*Go forra'd, Bones.*"
That's all he said, all the thanks I got—
    He got all the medals and rewards
For they gave him a pension and honorable mention
    And half a dozen ornamental swords.

Caldwell of Springfield [1780]

BRET HARTE

Here's the spot. Look around you. Above on the height
Lay the Hessians encamped. By that church on the right
Stood the gaunt Jersey farmers. And here ran a wall,—
You may dig anywhere and you'll turn up a ball.
Nothing more. Grasses spring, waters run, flowers blow,
Pretty much as they did ninety-three years ago.

Nothing more, did I say? Stay one moment; you've heard
Of Caldwell, the parson, who once preached the Word
Down at Springfield? What, No? Come—that's bad; why he had
All the Jerseys aflame. And they gave him the name
Of the "rebel high-priest." He stuck in their gorge,
For he loved the Lord God,—and he hated King George!

He had cause, you might say! When the Hessians that day
Marched up with Knyphausen they stopped on their way
At the "Farms," where his wife, with a child in her arms,
Sat alone in the house. How it happened none knew
But God—and that one of the hireling crew
Who fired the shot! Enough!—there she lay,
And—Caldwell, the chaplain, her husband, away!

Did he preach—did he pray? Think of him as you stand
By the old church to-day;—think of him and his band
Of militant ploughboys! See the smoke and the heat
Of that reckless advance,—of that straggling retreat!
Keep the ghost of that wife, foully slain, in your view,—
And what could you, what should you, what would you do?

Why, just what he did! They were left in the lurch
For the want of more wadding. He ran to the church,
Broke the door, stripped the pews, and dashed out in the road
With his arms full of hymn-books and threw down his load
At their feet! Then above all the shouting and shots,
Rang his voice,— "Put Watts into 'em,— Boys, give 'em Watts!"

And they did. That is all. Grasses spring, flowers blow
Pretty much as they did ninety-three years ago.
You may dig anywhere and you'll turn up a ball,—
But not always a hero like this,—and that's all.

The Capture of Major André |1780|

ANONYMOUS

Come all you brave Americans and unto me give ear,
I'll sing you now a ditty that will your spirits cheer,
Concerning a young gentleman who went to Tarrytown,
Where he met a British officer, a man of high renown.

Then up stepped this young hero, John Paulding was his name,
Oh, tell us where you're going sir, and also whence you came;
I bear the British flag sir, up answered bold André,
I have a pass that takes me through, I have no time to stay.

Then others came around him and bid him to dismount,
Come, tell us where you're going, give us a strict account;
Young Paulding said, we are resolved that you shall ne'er pass by,
And soon the evidence did prove the prisoner a spy.

He begged for his liberty, he pled for his discharge,
And oftentimes he told them, if they'd set him at large,
Here's all the gold and silver I have laid up in store,
But when I reach the city I will send you ten times more.

We scorn this gold and silver you have laid up in store,
Van Wart and Paulding both did cry—you need not send us more;
He saw that his conspiracy would soon be brought to light,
He begg'd for pen and paper and asked for to write.

The story came to Arnold, commanding at the fort,
He called for the Vulture and sailed for New York,
Now Arnold to New York has gone, a-fighting for his king,
And left poor Major André on the gallows for to swing.

André was executed—he looked both meek and mild,
His face was fair and handsome, and pleasantly he smiled;
It moved each eye with pity and every heart there bled,
And everyone wished him released, and Arnold in his stead.

He was a man of honor, in Britain he was born,
To die upon the gallows most highly he did scorn.
And now his life has reached its end, so young and blooming still,
In Tappan's quiet countryside he sleeps upon the hill.

Song of Marion's Men [1780–1781]

WILLIAM CULLEN BRYANT

Our band is few, but true and tried,
   Our leader frank and bold;
The British soldier trembles
   When Marion's name is told.
Our fortress is the good greenwood,
   Our tent the cypress-tree;
We know the forest round us
   As seamen know the sea.
We know its walls of thorny vines,
   Its glades of reedy grass,
Its safe and silent islands
   Within the dark morass.

Woe to the English soldiery
   That little dread us near!
On them shall light at midnight
   A strange and sudden fear:
When, waking to their tents on fire,
   They grasp their arms in vain,
And they who stand to face us
   Are beat to earth again;
And they who fly in terror deem
   A mighty host behind,
And hear the tramp of thousands
   Upon the hollow wind.

Then sweet the hour that brings release
   From danger and from toil;
We talk the battle over,
   We share the battle's spoil.
The woodland rings with laugh and shout,
   As if a hunt were up,
And woodland flowers are gathered
   To crown the soldier's cup.
With merry songs we mock the wind
   That in the pine-top grieves,
And slumber long and sweetly
   On beds of oaken leaves.

Well knows the fair and friendly moon
  The band that Marion leads—
The glitter of their rifles,
  The scampering of their steeds.
'Tis life to guide the fiery barb
  Across the moonlight plain;
'Tis life to feel the night-wind
  That lifts his tossing mane.
A moment in the British camp—
  A moment—and away,
Back to the pathless forest
  Before the peep of day.

Grave men there are by broad Santee,
  Grave men with hoary hairs;
Their hearts are all with Marion,
  For Marion are their prayers.
And lovely ladies greet our band
  With kindliest welcoming,
With smiles like those of summer.
  And tears like those of spring.
For them we wear these trusty arms,
  And lay them down no more
Till we have driven the Briton
  Forever from our shore.

Aaron Burr's Wooing

EDMUND CLARENCE STEDMAN

From the commandant's quarters on Westchester height
The blue hills of Ramapo lie in full sight;
On their slope gleam the gables that shield his heart's queen,
But the redcoats are wary—the Hudson's between.
Through the camp runs a jest: "There's no moon—'twill be dark;
'Tis odds little Aaron will go on a spark!"
And the toast of the troopers is: "Pickets, lie low,
And good luck to the colonel and Widow Prevost!"

Eight miles to the river he gallops his steed,
Lays him bound in the barge, bids his escort make speed,
Loose their swords, sit athwart, through the fleet reach yon shore.
Not a word—not a plash of the thick-muffled oar!
Once across, once again in the seat and away—
Five leagues are soon over when love has the say;
And "Old Put" and his rider a bridle-path know
To the Hermitage manor of Madame Prevost.

Lightly done! but he halts in the grove's deepest glade,
Ties his horse to a birch, trims his cue, slings his blade,
Wipes the dust and the dew from his smooth, handsome face,
With the 'kerchief she broidered and bordered in lace;
Then slips through the box-rows and taps at the hall,
Sees the glint of a waxlight, a hand white and small,
And the door is unbarred by herself all aglow—
Half in smiles, half in tears—Theodosia Prevost.

Alack for the soldier that's buried and gone!
What's a volley above him, a wreath on his stone,
Compared with sweet life and a wife for one's view
Like this dame, ripe and warm in her India fichu?
She chides her bold lover, yet holds him more dear,
For the daring that brings him a night-rider here;
British gallants by day through her doors come and go,
But a Yankee's the winner of Theo. Prevost.

Where's the widow or maid with a mouth to be kist,
When Burr comes a-wooing, that long would resist?
Lights and wine on the beaufet, the shutters all fast.
And "Old Put" stamps in vain till an hour has flown past—
But an hour, for eight leagues must be covered ere day;
Laughs Aaron, "Let Washington frown as he may,
When he hears of me next, in a raid on the foe,
He'll forgive this night's tryst with the Widow Prevost!"

Carmen Bellicosum

GUY HUMPHREY MCMASTER

In their ragged regimentals
Stood the old Continentals,
   Yielding not,
When the grenadiers were lunging,
And like hail fell the plunging
   Cannon-shot;
   When the files
   Of the isles,
From the smoky night-encampment, bore the banner of the rampant
   Unicorn;
And grummer, grummer, grummer, rolled the roll of the drummer
   Through the morn!

Then with eyes to the front all,
And with guns horizontal,
   Stood our sires;
And the balls whistled deadly,
And in streams flashing redly
   Blazed the fires:
   As the roar
   On the shore
Swept the strong battle-breakers o'er the green-sodded acres
   Of the plain;
And louder, louder, louder, cracked the black gunpowder,
   Cracking amain!

Now like smiths at their forges
Worked the red St. George's
   Cannoneers,
And the villainous saltpetre
Rung a fierce, discordant metre
   Round their ears;
   As the swift
   Storm-drift,
With hot sweeping anger, came the horse-guards' clangor
   On our flanks.
Then higher, higher, higher, burned the old-fashioned fire
   Through the ranks!

Then the bare-headed Colonel
Galloped through the white infernal
        Powder-cloud;
And his broadsword was swinging,
And his brazen throat was ringing
        Trumpet-loud;
        Then the blue
        Bullets flew,
And the trooper-jackets redden at the touch of the leaden
        Rifle-breath;
And rounder, rounder, rounder, roared the iron six-pounder,
        Hurling death!

Cornwallis' Country Dance [1781]

ANONYMOUS

Cornwallis led a country dance,
   The like was never seen, sir,
Much retrograde and much advance,
   And all with General Greene, sir.

They rambled up and rambled down,
   Joined hands, then off they run, sir
Our General Greene to Charlestown,
   The earl to Wilmington, sir.

Greene in the South then danced a set,
   And got a mighty name, sir,
Cornwallis jigged with young Fayette
   But suffered in his fame, sir.

Then down he figured to the shore,
   Most like a lordly dancer,
And on his courtly honor swore
   He would no more advance, sir.

Quoth he, my guards are weary grown
   With footing country dances,
They never at St. James's shone,
   At capers, kicks, or prances.

Though men so gallant ne'er were seen,
   While sauntering on parade, sir,
Or wriggling o'er the park's smooth green,
   Or at a masquerade, sir.

Yet are red heels and long-laced skirts,
   For stumps and briars meet, sir?
Or stand they chance with hunting-shirts,
   Or hardy veteran feet, sir?

Now housed in York, he challenged all,
   At minuet or all 'amande,
And lessons for a courtly ball
   His guards by day and night conned.

This challenge known, full soon there came
　　A set who had the bon ton,
De Grasse and Rochambeau, whose fame
　　Fut brillant pour un long tems.

And Washington, Columbia's son,
　　Whom easy nature taught, sir,
That grace which can't by pains be won,
　　Or Plutus's gold be bought, sir.

Now hand in hand they circle round
　　This ever-dancing peer, sir;
Their gentle movements soon confound
　　The Earl as they draw near, sir.

His music soon forgets to play—
　　His feet can move no more, sir,
And all his bands now curse the day
　　They jigged to our shore, sir.

Now Tories all, what can ye say?
　　Come—is not this a griper,
That while your hopes are danced away,
　　'Tis you must pay the piper?

Eutaw Springs [1781]

PHILIP FRENEAU

At Eutaw Springs the valiant died:
    Their limbs with dust are covered o'er;
Weep on, ye springs, your tearful tide;
    How many heroes are no more!

If in this wreck of ruin they
    Can yet be thought to claim a tear,
O smite thy gentle breast, and say
    The friends of freedom slumber here!

Thou, who shalt trace this bloody plain,
    If goodness rules thy generous breast,
Sigh for the wasted rural reign;
    Sigh for the shepherds sunk to rest!

Stranger, their humble graves adorn;
    You too may fall, and ask a tear:
'Tis not the beauty of the morn
    That proves the evening shall be clear.

They saw their injured country's woe,
    The flaming town, the wasted field;
Then rushed to meet the insulting foe;
    They took the spear—but left the shield.

Led by thy conquering standards, Greene,
    The Britons they compelled to fly:
None distant viewed the fatal plain,
    None grieved in such a cause to die—

But, like the Parthians famed of old,
    Who, flying, still their arrows threw,
These routed Britons, full as bold,
    Retreated, and retreating slew.

Now rest in peace our patriot band;
    Though far from nature's limits thrown,
We trust they find a happier land,
    A brighter Phoebus of their own.

AMERICA

THE WAR OF 1812

Ye Parliament of England [1812]

ANONYMOUS

Ye Parliament of England, ye Lords and Commons too,
Consider well what you're about—what you're about to do.
For you're to war with Yankees and I'm sure you'll rue the day.
You roused the sons of Liberty in North Americay!

You first confined our commerce and said our ships shan't trade,
You next impressed our seamen and used them as your slaves.
You then insulted Rodgers while plowing o'er the main,
And had we not declared war, you'd have done it o'er again!

You thought our frigates were but few and Yankees could not fight,
Until brave Hull your Guerriere took and banished her from sight.
For you're to war with Yankees and I'm sure you'll rue the day.
You roused the sons of Liberty in North Americay!

The Star-Spangled Banner [1814]

FRANCIS SCOTT KEY

Oh, say, can you see, by the dawn's early light,
    What so proudly we hailed at the twilight's last gleaming?
Whose broad stripes and bright stars, thro' the clouds of the fight,
    O'er the ramparts we watched were so gallantly streaming?
And the rockets' red glare, the bombs bursting in air,
    Gave proof thro' the night that our flag was still there;
Oh, say, does that star-spangled banner yet wave
    O'er the land of the free, and the home of the brave?

On that shore dimly seen thro' the mists of the deep,
    Where the foe's haughty host in dread silence reposes,
What is that which the breeze, o'er the towering steep,
    As it fitfully blows, now conceals, now discloses?
Now it catches the gleam of the morning's first beam.
    In full glory reflected now shines in the stream;
'Tis the star-spangled banner; oh, long may it wave
    O'er the land of the free, and the home of the brave!

And where is that band who so vauntingly swore,
    Mid the havoc of war and the battle's confusion,
A home and a country they'd leave us no more?
    Their blood has washed out their foul footsteps' pollution.
No refuge could save the hireling and slave
    From terror of flight or the gloom of the grave;
And the star-spangled banner in triumph doth wave
    O'er the land of the free, and the home of the brave.

Oh! thus be it ever, when freemen shall stand
    Between their loved home, and the war's desolation!
Blest with victory and peace, may the heav'n-rescued land
    Praise the Power that made and preserved us a nation.
Then conquer we must, when our cause it is just,
    And this be our motto, "*In God is our trust!*"
And the star-spangled banner in triumph shall wave
    O'er the land of the free, and the home of the brave.

The Warship of 1812

ANONYMOUS

She was no armored cruiser of twice six thousand tons,
With the thirty foot of metal that make your modern guns;
She didn't have a free board of thirty foot in clear,
An' she didn't need a million repairin' fund each year.
She had no rackin' engines to ramp an' stamp an' strain,
To work her steel-clad turrets an' break her hull in twain;
She did not have electric lights,—the battle-lantern's glare
Was all the light the 'tween decks had,—an' God's own good fresh air.

She had no gapin' air-flumes to throw us down our breath,
An' we didn't batten hatches to smother men to death;
She didn't have five hundred smiths—two hundred men would do—
In the old-time Yankee frigate for an old-time Yankee crew,
An' a fightin' Yankee captain, with his old-time Yankee clothes.
A-cursin' Yankee sailors with his old-time Yankee oaths.
She was built of Yankee timber and manned by Yankee men,
An' fought by Yankee sailors—Lord send their like again!

With the wind abaft the quarter and the sea foam flyin' free,
An' every tack and sheet housed taut and braces eased to lee,
You could hear the deep sea thunder from the knightheads where it broke,
As she trailed her lee guns under a blindin' whirl o' smoke.

She didn't run at twenty knots,—she wasn't built to run,—
An' we didn't need a half a watch to handle every gun.
Our captain didn't fight his ship from a little pen o' steel;
He fought her from his quarter-deck, with two hands at the wheel,
An' we fought in Yankee fashion, half naked,—stripped to board,—
An' when they hauled their red flag down we praised the Yankee Lord.
We fought like Yankee sailors, an' we'll do it, too, again;
You've changed the ships an' methods, but you can't change Yankee men!

The Constitution*'s Last Fight* [1815]

JAMES JEFFREY ROCHE

A Yankee ship and a Yankee crew—
    Constitution, where ye bound for?
Wherever, my lad, there's fight to be had
    Acrost the Western ocean.

Our captain was married in Boston town
    And sailed next day to sea;
For all must go when the State says so;
    Blow high, blow low, sailed we.

"Now, what shall I bring for a bridal gift
    When my home-bound pennant flies?
The rarest that be on land or sea
    It shall be my lady's prize."

"There's never a prize on sea or land
    Could bring such joy to me
As my true love sound and homeward bound
    With a king's ship under his lee."

The Western ocean is wide and deep,
    And wild its tempests blow,
But bravely rides *Old Ironsides*,
    A-cruising to and fro.

We cruised to the east and we cruised to north,
    And southing far went we,
And at last off Cape de Verd we raised
    Two frigates sailing free.

Oh, God made man, and man made ships,
    But God makes very few
Like him who sailed our ship that day,
    And fought her, one to two.

He gained the weather gauge of both,
    He held them both a-lee;
And gun for gun, till set of sun,
    He spoke them fair and free;

Till the night fog fell on spar and sail,
  And ship, and sea, and shore,
And our only aim was the bursting flame
  And the hidden cannon's roar.

Then a long rift in the mist showed up
  The stout *Cyane* close-hauled
To swing in our wake and our quarter rake,
  And a boasting Briton bawled:

"Starboard and larboard, we've got him fast
  Where his heels won't take him through;
Let him luff or wear, he'll find us there,—
  Ho, Yankee, which will you do?"

We did not luff and we did not wear,
  But braced our topsails back,
Till the sternway drew us fair and true
  Broadsides athwart her track.

Athwart her track and across her bows
  We raked her fore and aft,
And out of the fight and into the night
  Drifted the beaten craft.

The slow *Levant* came up too late;
  No need had we to stir;
Her decks we swept with fire, and kept
  The flies from troubling her.

We raked her again, and her flag came down,—
  The haughtiest flag that floats,—
And the lime-juice dogs lay there like logs,
  With never a bark in their throats.

With never a bark and never a bite,
  But only an oath to break,
As we squared away for Prava Bay
  With our prizes in our wake.

Parole they gave and parole they broke,
  What matters the cowardly cheat,
If the captain's bride was satisfied
  With the one prize laid at her feet?

A Yankee ship and a Yankee crew—
  Constitution, where ye bound for?
Wherever the British prizes be,
Though it's one to two, or one to three,—
Old Ironsides means victory,
  Acrost the Western ocean.

Ballad of New Orleans [1815]

CHARLES G. WILSON

Sir Edward Michael Pakenham
  And his most gracious Lady,
Came sailing into New Orleans
With ten thousand foot and the Royal Marines
To drive out the Yanks in their butternut jeans,
  And rule there with his Lady.

Andy Jackson lay stretched on his bed—
  For he was sick and ailing—
Old Hickory was sore beset,
His troops were green and their noses wet,
They hadn't been properly blooded yet,
  When the British came a-sailing.

Andy Jackson sprang from his bed
  And whistled his whelps together:
Long-haired men from the Tennessee,
French cadets in their filigree,
Coffee's irregular cavalry,
  And Kentucky men in leather.

Old Hickory rode down the line—
  The fog hung low like a pall—
Each lad lay prone in the woodsman's lore,
Until sudden a screaming rocket tore,
And the guns of the Fleet began to roar
  As Cochrane opened the ball.

The Yankee gunners touched the match
  And gave them ball for ball;
The long ships' guns of Dominique You,
Jean Lafitte and his pirate crew—
The heavens shook with their sulphurous spew,
  By the Rodriguez Canal.

A light wind whipped the fog to shreds
  And the sun came tumbling out.
Like a field of red the British came
In their splendid coats of scarlet flame,

Jogging along like lads at a game—
    On they came with a shout.

Andy Jackson passed the word—
    His voice was like musketfire:
"Hold your beads where the white belts cross!"
He watched the pulsing bayonets toss,
Grimly he reckoned the terrible loss . . .
    "Hold hard . . . hold hard . . . now fire!"

"Fire!" and a sheet of orange flame
    Leapt from the parapet,
The scarlet lines reeled under the stroke,
Formed up again in the stinking smoke,
Came charging on, and again they broke—
    The field lay red and wet.

With swinging kilts the Scots came down
    Across the bloodstained stubble:
The blasting grapeshot rutted their ranks,
The rifles tore at their quivering flanks,
Still on they came on their hairy shanks—
    Charging in at the double.

The buckskin boys lay cheek by jowl
    And cut them down like grain:
The Royal Marines and the Pioneers,
Wellington's veterans and Fusiliers,
And the pious praying Highlanders—
    They fell like the ripe, ripe grain.

Andy Jackson rode to town,
    Back to New Orleans,
With his French cadets in their filligree,
With Coffee's dismounted cavalry,
The Dirty Shirts from the Tennessee,
    And Kaintocks in their scalp-fringed jeans.

Sir Edward Michael Pakenham
    Sailed off with his gracious Lady:
He was coffined tight in a hogshead of rum,
His eyes were blind and his lips were dumb,
And his heart was as quiet as a bursted drum . . .
    God save his gracious Lady.

Hunters of Kentucky [1815]

ANONYMOUS

Ye gentlemen and ladies fair who grace this famous city,
Just listen, if you've time to spare, while I rehearse a ditty.
And for the opportunity concede yourselves quite lucky,
For 'tis not often that you see a hunter from Kentucky.
  Oh Kentucky, ye Hunters of Kentucky.

I 'spose you've read it in the prints how Pakenham attempted
To make old Hickory Jackson wince, but soon his scheme repented.
So Packenham he made his brags, if he in fight was lucky,
He'd have our gals, and cotton bags in spite of old Kentucky.
  Oh Kentucky, ye Hunters of Kentucky.

Old Jackson led us to the swamp, the ground was low and mucky;
There stood John Bull in martial pomp, and here was old Kentucky.
But steady stood our little force, none wished it to be greater,
For every man was half a horse and half an alligator.
  Oh Kentucky, ye Hunters of Kentucky.

And when so near we saw them wink, we thought it time to stop 'em.
It would have done you good, I think, to see Kentuckians drop 'em.
And now, if danger e'er annoys, remember what our trade is.
Just send for us Kentucky boys, and we'll protect ye, ladies!
  Oh Kentucky, ye Hunters of Kentucky.

AMERICA

THE WAR BETWEEN THE STATES

Battle-Hymn of the Republic [1861]

JULIA WARD HOWE

Mine eyes have seen the glory of the coming of the Lord:
He is trampling out the vintage where the grapes of wrath are stored;
He hath loosed the fateful lightning of his terrible swift sword:
 His truth is marching on.

I have seen Him in the watch-fires of a hundred circling camps;
They have builded Him an altar in the evening dews and damps;
I have read His righteous sentence by the dim and flaring lamps.
 His day is marching on.

I have read a fiery gospel, writ in burnished rows of steel:
"As ye deal with my contemners, so with you my grace shall deal;
Let the Hero, born of woman, crush the serpent with his heel,
 Since God is marching on."

He has sounded forth the trumpet that shall never call retreat;
He is sifting out the hearts of men before his judgment-seat:
Oh! be swift, my soul, to answer Him, be jubilant, my feet!
 Our God is marching on.

In the beauty of the lilies Christ was born across the sea,
With a glory in his bosom that transfigures you and me:
As he died to make men holy, let us die to make men free,
 While God is marching on.

The Bonnie Blue Flag [1861]

ANNIE CHAMBERS KETCHAM

We are a band of brothers, and native to the soil,
Fighting for our liberty with treasure, blood and toil.
And when our rights were threatened, the cry rose near and far,
"Hurrah for the Bonnie Blue Flag that bears a single star!"

Hurrah! Hurrah! For Southern rights hurrah!
Hurrah! for the Bonnie Blue Flag that bears a single star!

As long as the Union was faithful to her trust,
Like friends and like brethren, kind we were and just;
But now, when Northern treachery attempts our rights to mar,
We hoist on high the Bonnie Blue Flag that bears a single star.

First gallant South Carolina nobly made the stand,
Then came Alabama and took her by the hand.
Next quickly Mississippi, Georgia, and Florida
All raised on high the Bonnie Blue Flag that bears a single star.

Ye men of valor gather round the banner of the right;
Texas and fair Louisiana join us in the fight.
Davis, our loved President, and Stephens statesmen are.
Now rally round the Bonnie Blue Flag that bears a single star!

And here's to brave Virginia, the Old Dominion State,
That with the young Confederacy at length has linked her fate.
Impelled by her example, now other states prepar'
To hoist on high the Bonnie Blue Flag that bears a single star.

Then here's to our Confederacy, strong we are and brave;
Like patriots of old we'll fight our heritage to save;
And rather than submit to shame, to die we would prefer,
So cheer for the Bonnie Blue Flag that bears a single star.

Then cheer, boys, cheer; raise a joyous shout,
For Arkansas and North Carolina now have both gone out.
And let another rousing cheer for Tennessee be given;
The single star of the Bonnie Blue Flag has grown to be eleven.

My *Maryland* [1861]

JAMES RYDER RANDALL

The despot's heel is on thy shore,
    Maryland!
His torch is at thy temple door,
    Maryland!
Avenge the patriotic gore
That flecked the streets of Baltimore,
And be the battle-queen of yore,
    Maryland, my Maryland!

Hark to an exiled son's appeal,
    Maryland!
My Mother State, to thee I kneel,
    Maryland!
For life and death, for woe and weal,
Thy peerless chivalry reveal,
And gird thy beauteous limbs with steel,
    Maryland, my Maryland!

Thou wilt not cower in the dust,
    Maryland!
Thy beaming sword shall never rust,
    Maryland!
Remember Carroll's sacred trust,
Remember Howard's warlike thrust,
And all thy slumberers with the just,
    Maryland, my Maryland!

Come! 'tis the red dawn of the day,
    Maryland!
Come with thy panoplied array,
    Maryland!
With Ringgold's spirit for the fray,
With Watson's blood at Monterey,
With fearless Lowe and dashing May,
    Maryland, my Maryland!

Dear Mother, burst the tyrant's chain,
    Maryland!

Virginia should not call in vain,
    Maryland!
She meets her sisters on the plain,—
"Sic Semper!" 'tis the proud refrain.
That baffles minions back amain,
    Maryland!
Arise in majesty again,
    Maryland, my Maryland!

Come! for thy shield is bright and strong,
    Maryland!
Come! for thy dalliance does thee wrong,
    Maryland!
Come to thine own heroic throng,
Stalking with Liberty along,
And chant thy dauntless slogan-song,
    Maryland, my Maryland!

I see the blush upon thy cheek,
    Maryland!
For thou wast ever bravely meek,
    Maryland!
But lo! there surges forth a shriek,
From hill to hill, from creek to creek,
Potomac calls to Chesapeake,
    Maryland, my Maryland!

Thou wilt not yield the Vandal toll,
    Maryland!
Thou wilt not crook to his control,
    Maryland!
Better the fire upon thee roll,
Better the shot, the blade, the bowl,
Than crucifixion of the soul,
    Maryland, my Maryland!

I hear the distant thunder hum,
    Maryland!
The Old Line's bugle, fife, and drum,
    Maryland!
She is not dead, nor deaf, nor dumb;
Huzza! she spurns the Northern scum!
She breathes! She burns! She'll come! She'll come!
    Maryland, my Maryland!

The Battle-Cry of Freedom

GEORGE F. ROOT

Yes, we'll rally 'round the flag, boys, we'll rally once again,
  Shouting the battle-cry of freedom;
We will rally from the hillside, we'll gather from the plain,
  Shouting the battle-cry of freedom.

  The Union forever, hurrah, boys, hurrah!
    Down with the traitor, up with the star,
  While we rally 'round the flag, boys, rally once again,
    Shouting the battle-cry of freedom.

We are springing to the call of our brothers gone before,
  Shouting the battle-cry of freedom,
And we'll fill the vacant ranks with a million freemen more,
  Shouting the battle-cry of freedom.

We will welcome to our numbers the loyal, true, and brave,
  Shouting the battle-cry of freedom,
And altho' they may be poor, not a man shall be a slave,
  Shouting the battle-cry of freedom.

So we're springing to the call from the East and from the West,
  Shouting the battle-cry of freedom,
And we'll hurl the rebel crew from the land we love the best,
  Shouting the battle-cry of freedom.

John Brown's Body [1861]

ANONYMOUS

John Brown's body lies a-mould'ring in the grave,
John Brown's body lies a-mould'ring in the grave,
John Brown's body lies a-mould'ring in the grave,
    His soul is marching on!

    Glory! Glory Hallelujah!
    Glory! Glory Hallelujah!
    Glory! Glory Hallelujah!
    His soul is marching on.

He's gone to be a soldier in the army of the Lord!
He's gone to be a soldier in the army of the Lord!
He's gone to be a soldier in the army of the Lord!
    His soul is marching on.

John Brown's knapsack is strapped upon his back.
John Brown's knapsack is strapped upon his back.
John Brown's knapsack is strapped upon his back.
    His soul is marching on.

His pet lambs will meet him on the way,
His pet lambs will meet him on the way,
His pet lambs will meet him on the way,
    And they'll go marching on.

They'll hang Jeff Davis to a sour apple tree,
They'll hang Jeff Davis to a sour apple tree,
They'll hang Jeff Davis to a sour apple tree,
    As they go marching on.

Now for the Union let's give three rousing cheers,
Now for the Union let's give three rousing cheers,
Now for the Union let's give three rousing cheers,
    As we go marching on.
        Hip, hip, hip, hip, Hurrah!

Dixie (*Battle-Hymn*) [1861]

ALBERT PIKE

Southrons, hear your country call you!
Up, lest worse than death befall you!
To arms! To arms! To arms, in Dixie!
Lo! all the beacon-fires are lighted,—
Let all hearts be now united!
 To arms! To arms! To arms, in Dixie!
  Advance the flag of Dixie!
   Hurrah! hurrah!

For Dixie's land we take our stand,
 And live or die for Dixie!
  To arms! To arms!
 And conquer peace for Dixie!
  To arms! To arms!
 And conquer peace for Dixie.

Hear the Northern thunders mutter!
Northern flags in South winds flutter!
Send them back your fierce defiance!
Stamp upon the accursed alliance!

Fear no danger! Shun no labor!
Lift up rifle, pike, and sabre!
Shoulder pressing close to shoulder,
Let the odds make each heart bolder!

How the South's great heart rejoices
At your cannons' ringing voices!
For faith betrayed, and pledges broken,
Wrongs inflicted, insults spoken.

Strong as lions, swift as eagles,
Back to their kennels hunt these beagles!
Cut the unequal bonds asunder!
Let them hence each other plunder!

Swear upon your country's altar
Never to submit or falter,
Till the spoilers are defeated,
Till the Lord's work is completed.

Halt not till our Federation
Secures among earth's powers its station!
Then at peace, and crowned with glory,
Hear your children tell the story!

If the loved ones weep in sadness,
Victory soon shall bring them gladness,—
      To arms!
Exultant pride soon banish sorrow,
Smiles chase tears away to-morrow.
    To arms! To arms! To arms, in Dixie!
      Advance the flag of Dixie!
        Hurrah! hurrah!

For Dixie's land we take our stand,
    And live or die for Dixie!
      To arms! To arms!
    And conquer peace for Dixie!
      To arms! To arms!
    And conquer peace for Dixie!

Three Hundred Thousand More [1861]

JAMES SLOAN GIBBONS

We are coming, Father Abraham, three hundred thousand more,
From Mississippi's winding stream and from New England's shore;
We leave our ploughs and workshops, our wives and children dear,
With hearts too full for utterance, with but a silent tear;
We dare not look behind us, but steadfastly before:
We are coming, Father Abraham, three hundred thousand more!

If you look across the hilltops that meet the northern sky,
Long moving lines of rising dust your vision may descry;
And now the wind, an instant, tears the cloudy veil aside,
And floats aloft our spangled flag in glory and in pride,
And bayonets in the sunlight gleam, and bands brave music pour:
We are coming, Father Abraham, three hundred thousand more!

If you look all up our valleys where the growing harvests shine,
You may see our sturdy farmer boys fast forming into line;
And children from their mothers' knees are pulling at the weeds,
And learning how to reap and sow against their country's needs;
And a farewell group stands weeping at every cottage door;
We are coming, Father Abraham, three hundred thousand more!

You have called us, and we're coming, by Richmond's bloody tide
To lay us down, for Freedom's sake, our brothers' bones beside,
Or from foul treason's savage grasp to wrench the murderous blade,
And in the face of foreign foes its fragments to parade.
Six hundred thousand loyal men and true have gone before:
We are coming, Father Abraham, three hundred thousand more!

Kearney at Seven Pines [1862]

EDMUND CLARENCE STEDMAN

So that soldierly legend is still on its journey,—
    That story of Kearney who knew not to yield!
'Twas the day when with Jameson, fierce Berry, and Birney,
    Against twenty thousand he rallied the field.
Where the red volleys poured, where the clamor rose highest,
    Where the dead lay in clumps through the dwarf oak and pine,
Where the aim from the thicket was surest and nighest,—
    No charge like Phil Kearney's along the whole line.

When the battle went ill, and the bravest were solemn,
    Near the dark Seven Pines, where we still held our ground,
He rode down the length of the withering column,
    And his heart at our war-cry leapt up with a bound.
He snuffed, like his charger, the wind of the powder,—
    His sword waved us on, and we answered the sign;
Loud our cheer as we rushed, but his laugh rang the louder:
    "There's the devil's own fun, boys, along the whole line!"

How he strode his brown steed! How we saw his blade brighten
    In the one hand still left,—and the reins in his teeth!
He laughed like a boy when the holidays heighten,
    But a soldier's glance shot from his visor beneath.
Up came the reserves to the mellay infernal,
    Asking where to go in,—through the clearing or pine?
"Oh, anywhere! Forward! 'Tis all the same, Colonel;
    You'll find lovely fighting along the whole line!"

Oh, evil the black shroud of night at Chantilly,
    That hid him from sight of his brave men and tried!
Foul, foul sped the bullet that clipped the white lily,
    The flower of our knighthood, the whole army's pride!
Yet we dream that he still—in that shadowy region
    Where the dead form their ranks at the wan drummer's sign—
Rides on, as of old, down the length of his legion,
    And the word still is Forward! along the whole line.

Barbara Frietchie [1862]

JOHN GREENLEAF WHITTIER

Up from the meadows rich with corn,
Clear in the cool September morn,

The clustered spires of Frederick stand
Green-walled by the hills of Maryland.

Round about them orchards sweep,
Apple and peach tree fruited deep,

Fair as the garden of the Lord
To the eyes of the famished rebel horde,

On that pleasant morn of the early fall
When Lee marched over the mountain wall,

Over the mountains winding down,
Horse and foot, into Frederick town.

Forty flags with their silver stars,
Forty flags with their crimson bars,

Flapped in the morning wind: the sun
Of noon looked down, and saw not one.

Up rose old Barbara Frietchie then,
Bowed with her fourscore years and ten;

Bravest of all in Frederick town,
She took up the flag the men hauled down.

In her attic window the staff she set,
To show that one heart was loyal yet.

Up the street came the rebel tread,
Stonewall Jackson riding ahead.

Under his slouched hat left and right
He glanced; the old flag met his sight.

"Halt!"—the dust-brown ranks stood fast.
"Fire!"—out blazed the rifle-blast.

It shivered the window, pane and sash;
It rent the banner with seam and gash.

Quick as it fell, from the broken staff
Dame Barbara snatched the silken scarf.

She leaned far out on the window-sill,
And shook it forth with a royal will.

"Shoot, if you must, this old gray head,
But spare your country's flag," she said.

A shade of sadness, a blush of shame,
Over the face of the leader came;

The nobler nature within him stirred
To life at that woman's deed and word:

"Who touches a hair of yon gray head
Dies like a dog! March on!" he said.

All day long through Frederick street
Sounded the tread of marching feet:

All day long that free flag tost
Over the heads of the rebel host.

Ever its torn folds rose and fell
On the loyal winds that loved it well;

And through the hill-gaps sunset light
Shone over it with a warm good-night.

Barbara Frietchie's work is o'er,
And the Rebel rides on his raids no more.

Honor to her! and let a tear
Fall, for her sake, on Stonewall's bier.

Over Barbara Frietchie's grave,
Flag of Freedom and Union, wave!

Peace and order and beauty draw
Round thy symbol of light and law;

And ever the stars above look down
On thy stars below in Frederick town!

Ascent of T. J. Jackson: A Soldier's Tale [1863]

A. N.

"Angel!" said the Heavenly Father, "I have called my servant Jackson,
I have called my servant Jackson to desert the fields of war:
I have called him from his legion, at the height of all his conquest,
I have called him to attend on me, and reasons had therefore.

"For it is the will of Heaven," said the Vision wreathed in brightness,
"That the newly born republic of the Southern Cross shall fall;
For it is the will of Heaven that the other side shall triumph,
And that can never be till Jackson hearkens to my call.

"He has heard the word I sent him, he is ready for the journey,
He is pining for the shady trees in bloody Chancellorsville;
Now do you, archangel, greet him, with a host of angels further,
And escort my worthy servant to my throne upon the hill."

With a wave of silent pinions, at the word of the All-Father,
Michael and his white companions have departed on their quest;
From the vague and azured regions, like a rain or like the zephyr,
They are winging to the bier where Stonewall Jackson takes his rest.

I'm an old irreverent soldier but you must not think I'm lying,
And you must not think I'm drunk when I report the following tale:
For the angels could not find him, no, they could not come on Jackson,
Though they wandered viewlessly about the meadow and the dale.

And they looked within his coffin, and they looked within his shrouding,
And they looked in all the haunts they knew that he had once held dear;
But they couldn't come upon him, and they couldn't do their errand,
And Michael finally allowed that it looked mighty queer.

"We have used our ablest efforts, yet we cannot do our mission."
He reported to the angels that awaited his command;
"There is nothing left us now to do but journey back to Heaven.
And tell our tale to Him who holds all fates within His hand."

And as silently departing from those dreadful fields of battle
As they had dropped upon them on their errand still undone.
The archangel and his cohorts beat the airs of higher blueness,
Pass the misty clouds again until the Gates of Joy are won.

And they walk the stainless pavement to the presence of the Father,
And suddenly in wonderment recoil before the Throne!
There is Jackson humbly kneeling: he has fooled the weary angels,
He has flanked the searching party, and come up to Heaven alone!

Stonewall Jackson's Way [1863]

JOHN WILLIAMSON PALMER

Come, stack arms, men! Pile on the rails,
    Stir up the camp-fire bright;
No growling if the canteen fails,
    We'll make a roaring night.
Here Shenandoah brawls along,
There burly Blue Ridge echoes strong,
To swell the Brigade's rousing song
    Of "Stonewall Jackson's Way."

We see him now—the queer slouched hat
    Cocked o'er his eye askew;
The shrewd, dry smile; the speech so pat,
    So calm, so blunt, so true.
The "Blue-light Elder" knows 'em well;
Says he, "That's Banks, he's fond of shell;
Lord save his soul! we'll give him—" well!
    That's "Stonewall Jackson's Way."

Silence! ground arms! kneel all! caps off.
    Old Massa's going to pray.
Strangle the fool that dares to scoff!
    Attention! it's his way.
Appealing from his native sod,
In *forma pauperis* to God:
"Lay bare Thine arm; stretch forth Thy Rod!
    Amen!" That's "Stonewall's Way."

He's in the saddle now. Fall in!
    Steady! the whole brigade!
Hill's at the ford, cut off; we'll win
    His way out, ball and blade!
What matter if our shoes are worn?
What matter if our feet are torn?
"Quick step! we're with him before morn!"
    That's "Stonewall Jackson's Way."

The sun's bright lances rout the mists
  Of morning, and, by George!
Here's Longstreet, struggling in the lists,
  Hemmed in an ugly gorge.
Pope and his Dutchmen, whipped before;
"Bay'nets and grape!" hear Stonewall roar;
"Charge, Stuart! Pay off Ashby's score!"
  In "Stonewall Jackson's Way."

Ah, Maiden! wait and watch and yearn
  For news of Stonewall's band!
Ah, Widow! read, with eyes that burn,
  That ring upon thy hand.
Ah, Wife! sew on, pray on, hope on;
Thy life shall not be all forlorn;
The foe had better ne'er been born
  That gets in "Stonewall's Way."

Sheridan's Ride | 1864 |

THOMAS BUCHANAN READ

Up from the South at break of day,
Bringing to Winchester fresh dismay,
The affrighted air with a shudder bore,
Like a herald in haste, to the chieftain's door,
The terrible grumble, and rumble, and roar,
Telling the battle was on once more,
And Sheridan twenty miles away.

And wider still those billows of war
Thundered along the horizon's bar;
And louder yet into Winchester rolled
The roar of that red sea uncontrolled,
Making the blood of the listener cold,
As he thought of the stake in that fiery fray,
And Sheridan twenty miles away.

But there is a road from Winchester town,
A good broad highway leading down;
And there, through the flush of the morning light,
A steed as black as the steeds of night
Was seen to pass, as with eagle flight,
As if he knew the terrible need;
He stretched away with his utmost speed;
Hills rose and fell; but his heart was gay,
With Sheridan fifteen miles away.

Still sprung from whose swift hoofs, thundering South,
The dust, like smoke from the cannon's mouth;
Or a trail of a comet, sweeping faster and faster,
Foreboding to traitors the doom of disaster.
The heart of the steed and the heart of the master
Were beating like prisoners assaulting their walls,
Impatient to be where the battle-field calls;
Every nerve of the charger was strained to full play,
With Sheridan only ten miles away.

Under his spurning feet the road
Like an arrowy Alpine river flowed,
And the landscape sped away behind
Like an ocean flying before the wind;
And the steed, like a bark fed with furnace ire,
Swept on with his wild eye full of fire.
But lo! he is nearing his heart's desire;
He is snuffing the smoke of the roaring fray,
With Sheridan only five miles away.

The first that the General saw were the groups
Of stragglers, and then the retreating troops.
What was done? what to do? A glance told him both.
Then, striking his spurs, with a terrible oath,
He dashed down the line, mid a storm of huzzas,
And the wave of retreat checked its course there, because
The sight of the master compelled it to pause.
With foam and with dust the black charger was gray;
By the flash of his eye, and the red nostril's play,
He seemed to the whole great army to say,
"I have brought you Sheridan all the way
From Winchester down to save the day!"

Hurrah! hurrah for Sheridan!
Hurrah! hurrah for horse and man!
And when their statues are placed on high,
Under the dome of the Union sky,
The American soldier's Temple of Fame,—
There with the glorious General's name,
Be it said, in letters both bold and bright,
"Here is the steed that saved the day
By carrying Sheridan into the fight,
From Winchester, twenty miles away!"

The Blue and the Gray

FRANCIS MILES FINCH

By the flow of the inland river,
    Whence the fleets of iron have fled,
Where the blades of the grave-grass quiver,
    Asleep are the ranks of the dead:
        Under the sod and the dew,
            Waiting the judgment-day;
        Under the one, the Blue,
            Under the other, the Gray.

These in the robings of glory,
    Those in the gloom of defeat,
All with the battle-blood gory,
    In the dusk of eternity meet:
        Under the sod and the dew,
            Waiting the judgment-day;
        Under the laurel, the Blue,
            Under the willow, the Gray.

From the silence of sorrowful hours
    The desolate mourners go,
Lovingly laden with flowers
    Alike for the friend and the foe:
        Under the sod and the dew,
            Waiting the judgment-day;
        Under the roses, the Blue,
            Under the lilies, the Gray.

So with an equal splendor
    The morning sun-rays fall,
With a touch impartially tender,
    On the blossoms blooming for all:
        Under the sod and the dew,
            Waiting the judgment-day;
        Broidered with gold, the Blue,
            Mellowed with gold, the Gray.

So, when the summer calleth,
　　On forest and field of grain,
With an equal murmur falleth
　　The cooling drip of the rain:
　　　　Under the sod and the dew,
　　　　　　Waiting the judgment-day;
　　　　Wet with the rain, the Blue,
　　　　　　Wet with the rain, the Gray.

Sadly, but not with upbraiding,
　　The generous deed was done,
In the storm of the years that are fading,
　　No braver battle was won:
　　　　Under the sod and the dew,
　　　　　　Waiting the judgment-day;
　　　　Under the blossoms, the Blue,
　　　　　　Under the garlands, the Gray.

No more shall the war cry sever,
　　Or the winding rivers be red;
They banish our anger forever
　　When they laurel the graves of our dead!
　　　　Under the sod and the dew,
　　　　　　Waiting the judgment-day;
　　　　Love and tears for the Blue,
　　　　　　Tears and love for the Gray.

O Captain! My Captain! [1865]

WALT WHITMAN

O Captain! my Captain! our fearful trip is done;
The ship has weather'd every rack, the prize we sought is won;
The port is near, the bells I hear, the people all exulting,
While follow eyes the steady keel, the vessel grim and daring:
    But O heart! heart! heart!
        O the bleeding drops of red,
            Where on the deck my Captain lies,
            Fallen cold and dead!

O Captain! my Captain! rise up and hear the bells;
Rise up—for you the flag is flung—for you the bugle trills;
For you bouquets and ribbon'd wreaths—for you the shores a-crowding;
For you they call, the swaying mass, their eager faces turning;
    Here Captain! dear father!
        This arm beneath your head:
            It is some dream that on the deck
            You've fallen cold and dead.

My Captain does not answer, his lips are pale and still;
My father does not feel my arm, he has no pulse nor will:
The ship is anchor'd safe and sound, its voyage closed and done;
From fearful trip the victor ship comes in with object won:
    Exult, O shores, and ring, O bells!
        But I, with mournful tread,
            Walk the deck my Captain lies,
            Fallen cold and dead.

AMERICA

OTHER POEMS

America

S. F. SMITH

My country, 'tis of thee,
Sweet Land of Liberty,
   Of thee I sing;
Land where my fathers died,
Land of the pilgrims' pride,
From every mountain-side
   Let Freedom ring.

My native country, thee,
Land of the noble free,—
   Thy name I love;
I love thy rocks and rills,
Thy woods and templed hills,
My heart with rapture thrills
   Like that above.

Let music swell the breeze,
And ring from all the trees,
   Sweet Freedom's song;
Let mortal tongues awake;
Let all that breathe partake;
Let rocks their silence break,—
   The sound prolong.

Our fathers' God, to Thee,
Author of Liberty,
   To Thee I sing;
Long may our land be bright
With Freedom's holy light;
Protect us by Thy might,
   Great God, our King.

Columbus [1492]

JOAQUIN MILLER

Behind him lay the gray Azores,
  Behind the Gates of Hercules;
Before him not the ghost of shores,
  Before him only shoreless seas.
The good mate said: "Now must we pray,
  For lo! the very stars are gone.
Brave Admiral, speak, what shall I say?"
  "Why, say, 'Sail on! sail on! and on!' "

"My men grow mutinous day by day;
  My men grow ghastly wan and weak."
The stout mate thought of home; a spray
  Of salt wave washed his swarthy cheek.
"What shall I say, brave Admiral, say,
  If we sight naught but seas at dawn?"
"Why, you shall say at break of day,
  'Sail on! sail on! sail on! and on!' "

They sailed and sailed, as winds might blow,
  Until at last the blanched mate said:
"Why, now not even God would know
  Should I and all my men fall dead.
These very winds forget their way,
  For God from these dread seas is gone.
Now speak, brave Admiral, speak and say"—
  He said: "Sail on! sail on! and on!"

They sailed. They sailed. Then spake the mate:
   "This mad sea shows his teeth to-night.
He curls his lip, he lies in wait,
With lifted teeth, as if to bite!
Brave Admiral, say but one good word:
   What shall we do when hope is gone?"
The words leapt like a leaping sword:
   "Sail on! sail on! sail on! and on!"

Then, pale and worn, he kept his deck,
   And peered through darkness. Ah, that night
Of all dark nights! And then a speck—
   A light! A light! A light! A light!
It grew, a starlit flag unfurled!
   It grew to be Time's burst of dawn.
He gained a world; he gave that world
   Its grandest lesson: "On! sail on!"

The Pilgrim Fathers [1620]

JOHN PIERPONT

The Pilgrim Fathers,—where are they?
        The waves that brought them o'er
Still roll in the bay, and throw their spray
        As they break along the shore;
Still roll in the bay, as they rolled that day
        When the *Mayflower* moored below,
When the sea around was black with storms,
        And white the shore with snow.

The mists that wrapped the Pilgrim's sleep
        Still brood upon the tide;
And his rocks yet keep their watch by the deep
        To stay its waves of pride.
But the snow-white sail that he gave to the gale,
        When the heavens looked dark, is gone,—
As an angel's wing through an opening cloud
        Is seen, and then withdrawn.

The pilgrim exile,—sainted name!
        The hill whose icy brow
Rejoiced, when he came, in the morning's flame,
        In the morning's flame burns now.
And the moon's cold light, as it lay that night
        On the hillside and the sea,
Still lies where he laid his houseless head,—
        But the Pilgrim! where is he?

The Pilgrim Fathers are at rest:
 When summer's throned on high,
And the world's warm breast is in verdure drest,
 Go, stand on the hill where they lie.
The earliest ray of the golden day
 On that hallowed spot is cast;
And the evening sun, as he leaves the world,
 Looks kindly on that spot last.

The Pilgrim spirit has not fled:
 It walks in noon's broad light;
And it watches the bed of the glorious dead,
 With the holy stars by night.
It watches the bed of the brave who have bled,
 And still guards this ice-bound shore,
Till the waves of the bay, where the *Mayflower* lay,
 Shall foam and freeze no more.

The Landing of the Pilgrim Fathers in New England [1620]

FELICIA HEMANS

The breaking waves dashed high
  On a stern and rock-bound coast,
And the woods against a stormy sky
  Their giant branches tossed;

And the heavy night hung dark,
  The hills and waters o'er,
When a band of exiles moored their bark
  On the wild New England shore.

Not as the conqueror comes,
  They, the true-hearted, came;
Not with the roll of the stirring drums,
  And the trumpet that sings of fame;

Not as the flying come,
  In silence and in fear;
They shook the depths of the desert gloom
  With their hymns of lofty cheer.

Amidst the storm they sang,
  And the stars heard, and the sea;
And the sounding aisles of the dim woods rang
  To the anthem of the free.

The ocean eagle soared
  From his nest by the white waves' foam;
And the rocking pines of the forest roared—
  This was their welcome home.

There were men with hoary hair
    Amidst that pilgrim band:
Why had they come to wither there,
    Away from their childhood's land?

There was woman's fearless eye,
    Lit by her deep love's truth;
There was manhood's brow, serenely high,
    And the fiery heart of youth.

What sought they thus afar?
    Bright jewels of the mine?
The wealth of seas, the spoils of war?
    They sought a faith's pure shrine!

Ay, call it holy ground,
    The soil where first they trod;
They have left unstained what there they found—
    Freedom to worship God.

HEZEKIAH BUTTERWORTH

"Praise ye the Lord!" The psalm to-day
    Still rises on our ears,
Borne from the hills of Boston Bay
    Through five times fifty years,
When Winthrop's fleet from Yarmouth crept
    Out to the open main,
And through the widening waters swept,
    In April sun and rain.
      "Pray to the Lord with fervent lips,"
        The leader shouted, "pray;"
      And prayer arose from all the ships
        As faded Yarmouth Bay.

They passed the Scilly Isles that day,
    And May-days came, and June,
And thrice upon the ocean lay
    The full orb of the moon.
And as that day on Yarmouth Bay,
    Ere England sunk from view,
While yet the rippling Solent lay
    In April skies of blue,
      "Pray to the Lord with fervent lips"
        Each morn was shouted, "pray;"
      And prayer arose from all the ships,
        As first in Yarmouth Bay.

Blew warm the breeze o'er western seas,
    Through Maytime morns, and June,
Till hailed these souls the Isles of Shoals,
    Low 'neath the summer moon;
And as Cape Ann arose to view,
    And Norman's Woe they passed,
The wood-doves came the white mists through,
    And circled round each mast.
      "Pray to the Lord with fervent lips,"
        Then called the leader, "pray;"
      And prayer arose from all the ships,
        As first in Yarmouth Bay.

Above the sea the hill-tops fair—
　　God's towers—began to rise,
And odors rare breathed through the air,
　　Like the balms of Paradise.
Through burning skies the ospreys flew,
　　And near the pine-cooled shores
Danced airy boat and thin canoe,
　　To flash of sunlit oars.
　　　　"Pray to the Lord with fervent lips,"
　　　　　The leader shouted, "pray!"
　　　　Then prayer arose, and all the ships
　　　　　Sailed into Boston Bay.

The white wings folded, anchors down,
　　The sea-worn fleet in line,
Fair rose the hills where Boston town
　　Should rise from clouds of pine;
Fair was the harbor, summit-walled,
　　And placid lay the sea.
"Praise ye the Lord," the leader called;
　　"Praise ye the Lord," spake he.
　　　　"Give thanks to God with fervent lips,
　　　　　Give thanks to God to-day,"
　　　　The anthem rose from all the ships
　　　　　Safe moored in Boston Bay.

"Praise ye the Lord!" Primeval woods
　　First heard the ancient song,
And summer hills and solitudes
　　The echoes rolled along.
The Red Cross flag of England blew
　　Above the fleet that day,
While Shawmut's triple peaks in view
　　In amber hazes lay.
　　　　"Praise ye the Lord with fervent lips,
　　　　　Praise ye the Lord to-day,"
　　　　The anthem rose from all the ships
　　　　　Safe moored in Boston Bay.

The *Arabella* leads the song—
  The *Mayflower* sings below,
That erst the Pilgrims bore along
  The Plymouth reefs of snow.
Oh! never be that psalm forgot
  That rose o'er Boston Bay,
When Winthrop sang, and Endicott,
  And Saltonstall, that day:
    "Praise ye the Lord with fervent lips,
      Praise ye the Lord to-day;"
    And praise arose from all the ships,
      Like prayers in Yarmouth Bay.

That psalm our fathers sang we sing,
  That psalm of peace and wars,
While o'er our heads unfolds its wing
  The flag of forty starts
And while the nation finds a tongue
  For nobler gifts to pray,
'Twill ever sing the song they sung
  That first Thanksgiving Day!
    "Praise ye the Lord with fervent lips,
      Praise ye the Lord to-day;"
    So rose the song from all the ships,
      Safe moored in Boston Bay.

Our fathers' prayers have changed to psalms,
  As David's treasures old
Turned, on the Temple's giant arms,
  To lily-work of gold.
Ho! vanished ships from Yarmouth's tide,
  Ho! ships of Boston Bay,
Your prayers have crossed the centuries wide
  To this Thanksgiving Day!
    We pray to God with fervent lips,
      We praise the Lord to-day,
    As prayers arose from Yarmouth ships,
      But psalms from Boston Bay.

Hail, Columbia

JOSEPH HOPKINSON

Hail, Columbia! happy land!
Hail, ye heroes! heaven-born band!
Who fought and bled in Freedom's cause,
Who fought and bled in Freedom's cause,
And when the storm of war was gone,
Enjoyed the peace your valor won.
Let independence be your boast,
Ever mindful what it cost;
Ever grateful for the prize,
Let its altar reach the skies.

> *Firm, united, let us be,*
> *Rallying round our Liberty;*
> *As a band of brothers joined,*
> *Peace and safety we shall find.*

Immortal patriots! rise once more:
Defend your rights, defend your shore:
Let no rude foe, with impious hand,
Let no rude foe, with impious hand,
Invade the shrine where sacred lies
Of toil and blood the well-earned prize.
While offering peace, sincere and just,
In Heaven we place a manly trust,
That truth and justice will prevail,
And every scheme of bondage fail.

Sound, sound the trump of fame!
Let Washington's great name
Ring thro' the world with loud applause;
Ring thro' the world with loud applause;
Let every clime to Freedom dear
Listen with a joyful ear.
With equal skill, and godlike pow'r,
He governs in the fearful hour
Of horrid war, or guides with ease
The happier time of honest peace.

Behold the chief who now commands,
Once more to serve his country stands!
The rock on which the storm will beat,
The rock on which the storm will beat;
But armed in virtue, firm and true,
His hopes are fixed on Heaven and you.
When hope was sinking in dismay,
When glooms obscured Columbia's day,
His steady mind, from changes free,
Resolved on death or Liberty.

The American Flag

JOSEPH RODMAN DRAKE

When Freedom from her mountain height
   Unfurled her standard to the air,
She tore the azure robe of night,
   And set the stars of glory there.
She mingled with its gorgeous dyes
The milky baldric of the skies,
And striped its pure celestial white
With streakings of the morning light;
Then from his mansion in the sun
She called her eagle bearer down,
And gave into his mighty hand
The symbol of her chosen land.

Majestic monarch of the cloud,
   Who rear'st aloft thy regal form,
To hear the tempest trumpings loud
And see the lightning lances driven,
   When strive the warriors of the storm,
And rolls the thunder-drum of heaven,
Child of the sun! to thee 'tis given
   To guard the banner of the free,
To hover in the sulphur smoke,
To ward away the battle stroke,
And bid its blendings shine afar,
Like rainbows on the cloud of war,
   The harbingers of victory!

Flag of the brave! thy folds shall fly,
The sign of hope and triumph high,
When speaks the signal trumpet tone,
And the long line comes gleaming on.

Ere yet the life-blood, warm and wet,
Has dimmed the glistening bayonet,
Each soldier eye shall brightly turn
To where thy sky-born glories burn,
And, as his springing steps advance,
Catch war and vengeance from the glance.
And when the cannon-mouthings loud
Heave in wild wreaths the battle shroud,
And gory sabres rise and fall
Like shoots of flame on midnight's pall,
Then shall thy meteor glances glow,
    And cowering foes shall shrink beneath
Each gallant arm that strikes below
    That lovely messenger of death.

Flag of the seas! on ocean wave
Thy stars shall glitter o'er the brave;
When death, careering on the gale,
Sweeps darkly round the bellied sail,
And frighted waves rush wildly back
Before the broadside's reeling rack,
Each dying wanderer of the sea
Shall look at once to heaven and thee,
And smile to see thy splendors fly
In triumph o'er his closing eye.

Flag of the free heart's hope and home!
    By angel hands to valor given;
Thy stars have lit the welkin dome,
    And all thy hues were born in heaven.
Forever float that standard sheet!
    Where breathes the foe but falls before us,
With Freedom's soil beneath our feet,
    And Freedom's banner streaming o'er us?

The Flag Goes By

HENRY HOLCOMB BENNETT

Hats off!
Along the street there comes
A blare of bugles, a ruffle of drums;
A flash of color beneath the sky:
Hats off!
The flag is passing by!

Blue and crimson and white it shines,
Over the steel-tipped, ordered lines.
Hats off!
The colors before us fly;
But more than the flag is passing by.

Sea-fights and land-fights, grim and great,
Fought to make and save the State:
Weary marches and sinking ships;
Cheers of victory on dying lips;

Days of plenty and years of peace;
March of a strong land's swift increase;
Equal justice, right, and law,
Stately honor and reverend awe;

Sign of a nation, great and strong
To ward her people from foreign wrong
Pride and glory and honor,—all
Live in the colors to stand or fall.

Hats off!
Along the street there comes
A blare of bugles, a ruffle of drums;
And loyal hearts are beating high:
Hats off!
The flag is passing by!

"Old Ironsides"

OLIVER WENDELL HOLMES

Ay, tear her tattered ensign down!
    Long has it waved on high;
And many an eye has danced to see
    That banner in the sky;
Beneath it rung the battle shout,
    And burst the cannon's roar;—
The meteor of the ocean air
    Shall sweep the clouds no more.

Her deck, once red with heroes' blood,
    Where knelt the vanquished foe,
When winds were hurrying o'er the flood,
    And waves were white below,
No more shall feel the victor's tread,
    Or know the conquered knee;
The harpies of the shore shall pluck
    The eagle of the sea!

O, better that her shattered hulk
    Should sink beneath the wave;
Her thunders shook the mighty deep,
    And there should be her grave;
Nail to the mast her holy flag,
    Set every threadbare sail,
And give her to the god of storms.
    The lightning and the gale!

The Defence of the Alamo [1840]

JOAQUIN MILLER

Santa Ana came storming, as a storm might come;
　　There was rumble of cannon; there was rattle of blade;
There was cavalry, infantry, bugle, and drum,—
　　Full seven thousand, in pomp and parade,
The chivalry, flower of Mexico;
And a gaunt two hundred in the Alamo!

And thirty lay sick, and some were shot through;
　　For the siege had been bitter, and bloody, and long.
"Surrender, or die!"—"Men, what will you do?"
　　And Travis, great Travis, drew sword, quick and strong;
Drew a line at his feet . . . "Will you come? Will you go?
I die with my wounded, in the Alamo."

Then Bowie gasped, "Lead me over that line!"
　　Then Crockett, one hand to the sick, one hand to his gun,
Crossed with him; then never a word or a sign
　　Till all, sick or well, all, all save but one,
One man. Then a woman stepped, praying, and slow
Across; to die at her post in the Alamo.

Then that one coward fled, in the night, in that night
　　When all men silently prayed and thought
Of home; of to-morrow; of God and the right,
　　Till dawn: and with dawn came Travis's cannon shot,
In answer to insolent Mexico,
From the old bell-tower of the Alamo.

Then came Santa Ana; a crescent of flame!
　　Then the red "escalade"; then the fight hand to hand;
Such an unequal fight as never had name
　　Since the Persian hordes butchered that doomed Spartan band.
All day,—all day and all night, and the morning? so slow
Through the battle smoke mantling the Alamo.

Now silence! Such silence! Two thousand lay dead
    In a crescent outside! And within? Not a breath
Save the gasp of a woman, with gory gashed head,
    All alone, all alone there, waiting for death;
And she but a nurse. Yet when shall we know
Another like this of the Alamo?

Shout "Victory, victory, victory ho!"
    I say 'tis not always to the hosts that win;
I say that the victory, high or low,
    Is given the hero who grapples with sin,
Or legion or single; just asking to know
When duty fronts death in his Alamo.

Centennial Hymn [1876]

JOHN GREENLEAF WHITTIER

Our fathers' God! from out whose hand
The centuries fall like grains of sand,
We meet to-day, united, free,
And loyal to our land and Thee,
To thank Thee for the era done,
And trust Thee for the opening one.

Here, where of old, by Thy design,
The fathers spake that word of Thine
Whose echo is the glad refrain
Of rended bolt and falling chain,
To grace our festal time, from all
The zones of earth our guests we call.

Be with us while the New World greets
The Old World thronging all its streets,
Unveiling all the triumphs won
By art of toil beneath the sun,
And unto common good ordain
This rivalship of hand and brain.

Thou, who hast here in concord furled
The war flags of a gathered world,
Beneath our Western skies fulfil
The Orient's mission of good-will,
And, freighted with love's Golden Fleece,
Send back its Argonauts of peace.

For art and labor met in truce,
And beauty made the bride of use,
We thank Thee; but, withal, we crave
The austere virtues strong to save,
The honor proof to place or gold,
The manhood never bought nor sold!

Oh make Thou us, through centuries long,
In peace secure, in justice strong;
Around our gift of freedom draw
The safeguards of thy righteous law:
And, cast in some diviner mould,
Let the new cycle shame the old!

Columbia, the Gem of the Ocean

D. T. SHAW

O Columbia, the gem of the ocean,
   The home of the brave and the free,
The shrine of each patriot's devotion,
   A world offers homage to thee!
Thy mandates make heroes assemble,
   When Liberty's form stands in view;
Thy banners make Tyranny tremble,
   When borne by the red, white, and blue.

When borne by the red, white, and blue,
When borne by the red, white, and blue,
Thy banners make Tyranny tremble,
When borne by the red, white, and blue.

When war winged its wide desolation
   And threatened the land to deform,
The ark then of Freedom's foundation,
   Columbia, rode safe thro' the storm;
With her garlands of vict'ry around her,
   When so proudly she bore her brave crew,
With her flag proudly floating before her,
   The boast of the red, white, and blue.

The wine cup, the wine cup bring hither,
   And fill you it true to the brim;
May the wreaths they have won never wither,
   Nor the star of their glory grow dim!
May the service united ne'er sever,
   But they to their colors prove true!
The Army and Navy forever!
   Three cheers for the red, white, and blue!

The Republic

HENRY WADSWORTH LONGFELLOW

Thou, too, sail on, O Ship of State!
Sail on, O Union, strong and great!
Humanity with all its fears,
With all the hopes of future years,
Is hanging breathless on thy fate!
We know what Master laid thy keel,
What Workmen wrought thy ribs of steel,
Who made each mast, and sail, and rope,
What anvils rang, what hammers beat,
In what a forge and what a heat
Were shaped the anchors of thy hope!
Fear not each sudden sound and shock,
'Tis of the wave and not the rock;
'Tis but the flapping of the sail,
And not a rent made by the gale!
In spite of rock and tempest's roar,
In spite of false lights on the shore,
Sail on, nor fear to breast the sea!
Our hearts, our hopes, are all with thee,
Our hearts, our hopes, our prayers, our tears,
Our faith triumphant o'er our fears,
Are all with thee,—are all with thee!

Cuba Libre [1898]

JOAQUIN MILLER

Comes a cry from Cuban water—
    From the warm, dusk Antilles—
From the lost Atlanta's daughter,
    Drowned in blood as drowned in seas;
Comes a cry of purpled anguish—
    See her struggles, hear her cries!
Shall she live, or shall she languish?
    Shall she sink, or shall she rise?

She shall rise, by all that's holy!
    She shall live and she shall last;
Rise as we, when crushed and lowly,
    From the blackness of the past.
Bid her strike! Lo, it is written
    Blood for blood and life for life.
Bid her smite, as she is smitten;
    Stars and stripes were born of strife.

Once we flashed her lights of freedom,
    Lights that dazzled her dark eyes
Till she could but yearning heed them,
    Reach her hands and try to rise.
Then they stabbed her, choked her, drowned her
    Till we scarce could hear a note.
Ah! these rusting chains that bound her!
    Oh! these robbers at her throat!

And the kind who forged these fetters?
  Ask five hundred years for news.
Stake and thumbscrew for their betters!
  Inquisitions! Banished Jews!
Chains and slavery! What reminder
  Of one red man in that land?
Why, these very chains that bind her
  Bound Columbus, foot and hand!

Shall she rise as rose Columbus,
  From his chains, from shame and wrong—
Rise as Morning, matchless, wondrous—
  Rise as some rich morning song—
Rise a ringing song and story,
  Valor, Love personified?
Stars and stripes espouse her glory,
  Love and Liberty allied.

The White Man's Burden:
The United States and the Philippine Islands [1899]

RUDYARD KIPLING

Take up the White Man's burden—
    Send forth the best ye breed—
Go bind your sons to exile
    To serve your captives' need;
To wait in heavy harness
    On fluttered folk and wild—
Your new-caught, sullen peoples,
    Half devil and half child.

Take up the White Man's burden—
    In patience to abide,
To veil the threat of terror
    And check the show of pride;
By open speech and simple,
    An hundred times made plain.
To seek another's profit,
    And work another's gain.

Take up the White Man's burden—
    The savage wars of peace—
Fill full the mouth of Famine
    And bid the sickness cease;
And when your goal is nearest
    The end for others sought,
Watch Sloth and heathen Folly
    Bring all your hope to nought.

Take up the White Man's burden—
    No tawdry rule of kings,
But toil of serf and sweeper—
    The tale of common things.
The ports ye shall not enter,
    The roads ye shall not tread,
Go make them with your living,
    And mark them with your dead!

Take up the White Man's burden—
    And reap his old reward:
The blame of those ye better,
    The hate of those ye guard—
The cry of hosts ye humour
    (Ah, slowly!) toward the light:—
"Why brought ye us from bondage,
    Our loved Egyptian night?"

Take up the White Man's burden—
    Ye dare not stoop to less—
Nor call too loud on Freedom
    To cloak your weariness;
By all ye cry or whisper,
    By all ye leave or do,
The silent, sullen peoples
    Shall weigh your Gods and you.

Take up the White Man's burden—
    Have done with childish days—
The lightly proffered laurel,
    The easy, ungrudged praise.
Comes now, to search your manhood
    Through all the thankless years,
Cold-edged with dear-bought wisdom,
    The judgment of your peers!

The Marine Hymn

ANONYMOUS

From the halls of Montezuma
To the shores of Tripoli,
We fight our country's battles
On the land as on the sea;
First to fight for right and freedom
And to keep our honor clean;
We are proud to claim the title
Of United States Marine.

Our flag's unfurled to every breeze
From dawn to setting sun,
We have fought in every clime or place
Where we could take a gun:
In the snow of far off northern lands,
And in sunny tropic scenes,
You will find us always on the job,
The United States Marines.

Here's health to you and to our corps
Which we are proud to serve;
In many a strife we've fought for life,
And never lost our nerve.
If the Army and the Navy
Ever gaze on Heaven's scenes,
They will find the streets are guarded by
The United States Marines.

The Caissons Go Rolling Along

ANONYMOUS

Over hill, over dale,
We will hit the dusty trail,
And those caissons go rolling along.
Up and down, in and out,
Counter march and left about,
And those caissons go rolling along.
For it's high-high-he
In the Field Artillery,
Shout out your numbers loud and strong;
For where'er we go
You will always know
That those caissons go rolling along,
That those caissons go rolling along.

I Have a Rendezvous with Death [1917–1918]

ALAN SEEGER

I have a rendezvous with Death
At some disputed barricade,
When Spring comes round with rustling shade
And apple blossoms fill the air.
I have a rendezvous with Death
When Spring brings back blue days and fair.

It may be he shall take my hand
And lead me into his dark land
And close my eyes and quench my breath;
It may be I shall pass him still.
I have a rendezvous with Death
On some scarred slope of battered hill,
When Spring comes round again this year
And the first meadow flowers appear.

In Flanders Fields [1917–1918]

LIEUTENANT-COLONEL JOHN MCCRAE

In Flanders fields the poppies blow
Between the crosses, row on row,
   That mark our place; and in the sky
   The larks, still bravely singing, fly
Scarce heard amid the guns below.

We are the Dead. Short days ago
We lived, felt dawn, saw sunset glow,
   Loved and were loved, and now we lie
         In Flanders fields.

Take up our quarrel with the foe:
To you from failing hands we throw
   The torch; be yours to hold it high.
   If ye break faith with us who die
We shall not sleep, though poppies grow
         In Flanders fields.

Invocation *from* John Brown's Body

STEPHEN VINCENT BENET

American muse, whose strong and diverse heart
So many men have tried to understand
But only made it smaller with their art,
Because you are as various as your land,

As mountainous-deep, as flowered with blue rivers,
Thirsty with deserts, buried under snows.
As native as the shape of Navajo quivers,
And native, too, as the sea-voyaged rose.

Swift runner, never captured or subdued,
Seven-branched elk beside the mountain stream,
That half a hundred hunters have pursued
But never matched their bullets with the dream,

Where the great huntsmen failed, I set my sorry
And mortal snare for your immortal quarry.

You are the buffalo-ghost, the broncho-ghost
With dollar-silver in your saddle-horn,
The cowboys riding in from Painted Post,
The Indian arrow in the Indian corn,

And you are the clipped velvet of the lawns
Where Shropshire grows from Massachusetts sods,
The grey Maine rocks—and the war-painted dawns
That break above the Garden of the Gods.

The prairie-schooners crawling toward the ore
And the cheap car, parked by the station-door.

Where the skyscrapers lift their foggy plumes
Of stranded smoke out of a stony mouth
You are that high stone and its arrogant fumes,
And you are ruined gardens in the South

And bleak New England farms, so winter-white
Even their roofs look lonely, and the deep
The middle grainland where the wind of night
Is like all blind earth sighing in her sleep.

A friend, an enemy, a sacred hag
With two tied oceans in her medicine-bag.

They tried to fit you with an English song
And clip your speech into the English tale.
But, even from the first, the words went wrong,
The catbird pecked away the nightingale.

The homesick men begot high-cheekboned things
Whose wit was whittled with a different sound
And Thames and all the rivers of the kings
Ran into Mississippi and were drowned.

They planted England with a stubborn trust.
But the cleft dust was never English dust.

Stepchild of every exile from content
And all the disavouched, hard-bitten pack
Shipped overseas to steal a continent
With neither shirts nor honor to their back.

Pimping grandee and rump-faced regicide,
Apple-cheeked younkers from a windmill-square,
Puritans stubborn as the nails of Pride,
Rakes from Versailles and thieves from County Clare,

The black-robed priests who broke their hearts in vain
To make you God and France or God and Spain.

These were your lovers in your buckskin-youth.
And each one married with a dream so proud
He never knew it could not be the truth
And that he coupled with a girl of cloud.

And now to see you is more difficult yet
Except as an immensity of wheel
Made up of wheels, oiled with inhuman sweat
And glittering with the heat of ladled steel.

All these you are, and each is partly you,
And none is false, and none is wholly true.

So how to see you as you really are,
So how to suck the pure, distillate, stored
Essence of essence from the hidden star
And make it pierce like a riposting sword.

For, as we hunt you down, you must escape
And we pursue a shadow of our own
That can be caught in a magician's cape
But has the flatness of a painted stone.

Never the running stag, the gull at wing,
The pure elixir, the American thing.

And yet, at moments when the mind was hot
With something fierier than joy or grief,
When each known spot was an eternal spot
And every leaf was an immortal leaf,

I think that I have seen you, not as one,
But clad in diverse semblances and powers,
Always the same, as light falls from the sun,
And always different, as the differing hours.

Yet, through each altered garment that you wore
The naked body, shaking the heart's core.

All day the snow fell on that Eastern town
With its soft, pelting, little, endless sigh
Of infinite flakes that brought the tall sky down
Till I could put my hands in the white sky

And taste cold scraps of heaven on my tongue
And walk in such a changed and luminous light
As gods inhabit when the gods are young.
All day it fell. And when the gathered night

Was a blue shadow cast by a pale glow
I saw you then, snow-image, bird of the snow.

And I have seen and heard you in the dry
Close-huddled furnace of the city street
When the parched moon was planted in the sky
And the limp air hung dead against the heat.

I saw you rise, red as that rusty plant,
Dizzied with lights, half-mad with senseless sound,
Enormous metal, shaking to the chant
Of a triphammer striking iron ground.

Enormous power, ugly to the fool,
And beautiful as a well-handled tool.

These, and the memory of that windy day
On the bare hills, beyond the last barbed wire,
When all the orange poppies bloomed one way
As if a breath would blow them into fire,

I keep forever, like the sea-lion's tusk
The broken sailor brings away to land,
But when he touches it, he smells the musk,
And the whole sea lies hollow in his hand.

So, from a hundred visions, I make one,
And out of darkness build my mocking sun.

And should that task seem fruitless in the eyes
Of those a different magic sets apart
To see through the ice-crystal of the wise
No nation but the nation that is Art,

Their words are just. But when the birchbark-call
Is shaken with the sound that hunters make
The moose comes plunging through the forest-wall
Although the rifle waits beside the lake.

Art has no nations—but the mortal sky
Lingers like gold in immortality.

This flesh was seeded from no foreign grain
But Pennsylvania and Kentucky wheat,
And it has soaked in California rain
And five years tempered in New England sleet

To strive at last, against an alien proof
And by the changes of an alien moon,
To build again that blue, American roof
Over a half-forgotten battle-tune

And call unsurely, from a haunted ground,
Armies of shadows and the shadow-sound.

In your Long House there is an attic-place
Full of dead epics and machines that rust,
And there, occasionally, with casual face,
You come awhile to stir the sleepy dust;

Neither in pride nor mercy, but in vast
Indifference at so many gifts unsought,
The yellowed satins, smelling of the past,
And all the loot the lucky pirates brought.

I only bring a cup of silver air,
Yet, in your casualness, receive it there.

Receive the dream too haughty for the breast,
Receive the words that should have walked as bold
As the storm walks along the mountain-crest
And are like beggars whining in the cold.

The maimed presumption, the unskilful skill,
The patchwork colors, fading from the first,
And all the fire that fretted at the will
With such a barren ecstasy of thirst.

Receive them all—and should you choose to touch them
With one slant ray of quick, American light,
Even the dust will have no power to smutch them,
Even the worst will glitter in the night.

If not—the dry bones littered by the way
May still point giants toward their golden prey.

America the Beautiful

KATHERINE LEE BATES

O beautiful for spacious skies,
   For amber waves of grain,
For purple mountain majesties
   Above the fruited plain!
     America! America!
   God shed His grace on thee
And crown thy good with brotherhood
   From sea to shining sea!

O beautiful for pilgrim feet,
   Whose stern, impassioned stress
A thoroughfare for freedom beat
   Across the wilderness!
     America! America!
   God mend thine every flaw,
Confirm thy soul in self-control,
   Thy liberty in law!

O beautiful for heroes proved
   In liberating strife,
Who more than self their country loved,
   And mercy more than life!
     America! America!
   May God thy gold refine,
Till all success be nobleness,
   And every gain divine!

O beautiful for patriot dream
   That sees beyond the years
Thine alabaster cities gleam
   Undimmed by human tears!
     America! America!
   God shed His grace on thee!
And crown thy good with brotherhood
   From sea to shining sea!

ENGLAND

Battle of Brunanburh [937]

ALFRED, LORD TENNYSON

Athelstan King,
Lord among Earls,
Bracelet-bestower and
Baron of Barons,
He with his brother,
Edmund Atheling,
Gaining a lifelong
Glory in battle,
Slew with the sword-edge
There by Brunanburh,
Brake the shield-wall,
Hew'd the lindenwood,
Hack'd the battleshield,
Sons of Edward with hammer'd brands.

Theirs was a greatness
Got from their Grandsires—
Theirs that so often in
Strife with their enemies
Struck for their hoards and their hearths and their homes.

Bow'd the spoiler,
Bent the Scotsman,
Fell the shipcrews
Doom'd to the death.
All the field with blood of the fighters
Flow'd, from when first the great
Sun-star of morningtide,
Lamp of the Lord God
Lord everlasting,
Glode over earth till the glorious creature
Sunk to his setting.

There lay many a man
Marr'd by the javelin,
Men of the Northland
Shot over shield.
There was the Scotsman
Weary of war.

We the West-Saxons,
Long as the daylight
Lasted, in companies
Troubled the track of the host that we hated,
Grimly with swords that were sharp from the grindstone,
Fiercely we hack'd at the flyers before us.

Mighty the Mercian,
Hard was his hand-play,
Sparing not any of
Those that with Anlaf,
Warriors over the
Weltering waters
Borne in the bark's-bosom,
Drew to this island,
Doom'd to the death.

Five young kings put asleep by the sword-stroke,
Seven strong Earls of the army of Anlaf
Fell on the war-field, numberless numbers,
Shipmen and Scotsmen.

Then the Norse leader,
Dire was his need of it,
Few were his following,
Fled to his warship:
Fleeted his vessel to sea with the king in it,
Saving his life on the fallow flood.

Also the crafty one,
Constantinus,
Crept to his North again,
Hoar-headed hero!

Slender reason had
He to be proud of
The welcome of war-knives—
He that was reft of his
Folk and his friends that had
Fallen in conflict,
Leaving his son too
Lost in the carnage,
Mangled to morsels,
A youngster in war!

Slender reason had
He to be glad of
The clash of the war glaive
Traitor and trickster
And spurner of treaties—
He nor had Anlaf
With armies so broken
A reason for bragging
That they had the better
In perils of battle
On places of slaughter—
The struggle of standards,
The rush of the javelins,
The crash of the charges,
The wielding of weapons—
The play that they play'd with
The children of Edward.

Then with their nail'd prows
Parted the Norsemen, a
Blood-redden'd relic of
Javelins over
The jarring breaker, the deepsea billow,
Shaping their way toward Dyflen again,
Shamed in their souls.

Also the brethren,
King and Atheling,
Each in his glory,
Went to his own in his own West-Saxonland,
Glad of the war.

Many a carcase they left to be carrion,
Many a livid one, many a sallow-skin—
Left for the white-tail'd eagle to tear it, and
Left for the horny-nibb'd raven to rend it, and
Gave to the garbaging war-hawk to gorge it, and
That gray beast, the wolf of the weald.

Never had huger
Slaughter of heroes
Slain by the sword-edge—
Such as old writers
Have writ of in histories—
Hapt in this isle, since
Up from the East hither
Saxon and Angle from
Over the broad billow
Broke into Britain with
Haughty war-workers who
Harried the Welshman, when
Earls that were lured by the
Hunger of glory gat
Hold of the land.

England [1399]

WILLIAM SHAKESPEARE

This royal throne of kings, this scepter'd isle,
This earth of Majesty, this seat of Mars,
This older Eden, demi-paradise,
This fortress built by Nature for herself
Against infection and the hand of war,
This happy breed of men, this little world,
This precious stone set in the silver sea,
Which serves it in the office of a wall,
Or as a moat defensive to a house,
Against the envy of less happier lands,
This blessed plot, this earth, this realm, this England,
This nurse, this teeming womb of royal kings,
Fear'd by their breed and famous by their birth,
Renowned for their deeds as far from home,
For Christian service and true chivalry,
As is the sepulchre in stubborn Jewry
Of the world's ransom, blessed Mary's Son;
This land of such dear souls, this dear dear land,
Dear for her reputation through the world,
Is now leased out, I die pronouncing it,
Like to a tenement or pelting farm:
England, bound in with the triumphant sea,
Whose rocky shore beats back the envious siege
Of watery Neptune, is now bound in with shame,
With inky blots and rotten parchment bonds:
That England, that was wont to conquer others,
Hath made a shameful conquest of itself.
Ah, would the scandal vanish with my life,
How happy then were my ensuing death!

WILLIAM SHAKESPEARE

Once more unto the breach, dear friends, once more;
Or close the wall up with our English dead.
In peace there's nothing so becomes a man
As modest stillness and humility:
But when the blast of war blows in our ears,
Then imitate the action of the tiger;
Stiffen the sinews, summon up the blood,
Disguise fair nature with hard-favour'd rage;
Then lend the eye a terrible aspèct;
Let it pry through the portage of the head
Like the brass cannon; let the brow o'erwhelm it
As fearfully as doth a galled rock
O'erhang and jutty his confounded base,
Swill'd with the wild and wasteful ocean.
Now set the teeth and stretch the nostril wide,
Hold hard the breath and bend up every spirit
To his full height. On, on, you noblest English,
Whose blood is fet from fathers of war-proof!
Fathers that, like so many Alexanders,
Have in these parts from morn till even fought
And sheathed their swords for lack of argument:
Dishonour not your mothers; now attest
That those whom you call'd fathers did beget you.
Be copy now to men of grosser blood,
And teach them how to war. And you, good yeomen,
Whose limbs were made in England, show us here
The mettle of your pasture; let us swear
That you are worth your breeding; which I doubt not;
For there is none of you so mean and base,
That hath not noble lustre in your eyes.
I see you stand like greyhounds in the slips,
Straining upon the start. The game's afoot:
Follow your spirit, and upon this charge
Cry "God for Harry, England, and St. George!"

WILLIAM SHAKESPEARE

. . . He which hath no stomach to this fight,
Let him depart; his passport shall be made
And crowns for convoy put into his purse:
We would not die in that man's company
That fears his fellowship to die with us.
This day is call'd the feast of Crispian:
He that outlives this day, and comes safe home,
Will stand a tip-toe when this day is named,
And rouse him at the name of Crispian.
He that shall live this day, and see old age,
Will yearly on the vigil feast his neighbours,
And say "To-morrow is Saint Crispian:"
Then will he strip his sleeve and show his scars,
And say "These wounds I had on Crispin's day."
Old men forget; yet all shall be forgot,
But he'll remember with advantages
What feats he did that day: then shall our names,
Familiar in his mouth as household words,
Harry the king, Bedford and Exeter,
Warwick and Talbot, Salisbury and Gloucester,
Be in their flowing cups freshly remember'd.
This story shall the good man teach his son;
And Crispin Crispian shall ne'er go by,
From this day to the ending of the world,
But we in it shall be rememberèd;
We few, we happy few, we band of brothers;
For he to-day that sheds his blood with me
Shall be my brother; be he ne'er so vile,
This day shall gentle his condition:
And gentlemen in England now a-bed
Shall think themselves accursed they were not here,
And hold their manhoods cheap whiles any speaks
That fought with us upon Saint Crispin's day.

To the Cambrio-Britons and Their Harp,

His Ballad of Agincourt [1415]

MICHAEL DRAYTON

Fair stood the wind for France,
When we our sails advance,
Nor now to prove our chance
   Longer will tarry;
But putting to the main,
At Kaux, the mouth of Seine,
With all his martial train,
   Landed King Harry.

And taking many a fort,
Furnished in warlike sort,
Marchèd towards Agincourt
   In happy hour—
Skirmishing day by day
With those that stopped his way
Where the French gen'ral lay
   With all his power,

Which in his height of pride,
King Henry to deride,
His ransom to provide
   To the king sending;
Which he neglects the while,
As from a nation vile,
Yet, with an angry smile,
   Their fall portending.

And turning to his men,
Quoth our brave Henry then:
"Though they to one be ten,
   Be not amazed.
Yet have we well begun—
Battles so bravely won
Have ever to the sun
   By fame been raised.

"And for myself," quoth he,
"This my full rest shall be;
England ne'er mourn for me,
        Nor more esteem me.
Victor I will remain,
Or on this earth lie slain,
Never shall she sustain
        Loss to redeem me.

"Poitiers and Cressy tell,
When most their pride did swell,
Under our swords they fell;
        No less our skill is
Than when our grandsire great,
Claiming the regal seat,
By many a warlike feat
        Looped the French lilies."

The Duke of York so dread
The eager vaward led;
With the main Henry sped,
        Amongst his henchmen.
Excester had the rear—
A braver man not there:
O Lord! how hot they were
        On the false Frenchmen!

They now to fight are gone;
Armor on armor shone,
Drum now to drum did groan—
        To hear was wonder;
That with cries they make
The very earth did shake;
Trumpet to trumpet spake,
        Thunder to thunder.

Well it thine age became,
O noble Erpingham!
Which did the signal aim
        To our hid forces;
When, from a meadow by,
Like a storm suddenly,
The English archery
        Stuck the French horses,

With Spanish yew so strong,
Arrows a cloth-yard long,
That like to serpents stung,
    Piercing the weather;
None from his fellow starts,
But playing manly parts,
And like true English hearts,
    Stuck close together.

When down their bows they threw,
And forth their bilbows drew,
And on the French they flew,
    Not one was tardy:
Arms were from shoulders sent;
Scalps to the teeth were rent;
Down the French peasants went;
    Our men were hardy.

This while our noble king,
His broadsword brandishing,
Down the French host did ding,
    As to o'erwhelm it;
And many a deep wound lent,
His arms with blood besprent,
And many a cruel dent
    Bruised his helmet.

Glo'ster, that duke so good,
Next of the royal blood,
For famous England stood.
    With his brave brother.
Clarence,—in steel so bright,
Though but a maiden knight,—
Yet in that furious fight
    Scarce such another.

Warwick in blood did wade,
Oxford the foe invade,
And cruel slaughter made,
    Still as they ran up;
Suffolk his axe did ply;
Beaumont and Willoughby
Bare them right doughtily,
    Ferrers and Fanhope.

Upon Saint Crispin's day
Fought was this noble fray,
Which fame did not delay
    To England to carry;
Oh, when shall Englishmen
With such acts fill a pen,
Or England breed again
    Such a King Harry!

The Revenge [1591]

ALFRED, LORD TENNYSON

At Florès in the Azorès, Sir Richard Grenville lay,
And a pinnace, like a fluttered bird, came flying from far away:
"Spanish ships-of-war at sea! we have sighted fifty-three!"
Then sware Lord Thomas Howard: " 'Fore God I am no coward;
But I cannot meet them here, for my ships are out of gear,
And the half my men are sick. I must fly, but follow quick.
We are six ships of the line; can we fight with fifty-three?"

Then spake Sir Richard Grenville: "I know you are no coward;
You fly them for a moment to fight with them again.
But I've ninety men and more that are lying sick ashore.
I should count myself the coward if I left them, my Lord Howard,
To these Inquisition dogs and the devildoms of Spain."

So Lord Howard passed away with five ships of war that day,
Till he melted like a cloud in the silent summer heaven;
But Sir Richard bore in hand all his sick men from the land
     Very carefully and slow,
     Men of Bideford in Devon,
     And we laid them on the ballast down below;
     For we brought them all aboard,
And they blest him in their pain, that they were not left to Spain,
To the thumbscrew and the stake, for the glory of the Lord.

He had only a hundred seamen to work the ship and to fight,
And he sailed away from Florès till the Spaniard came in sight,
With his huge sea-castles heaving upon the weather bow.
     "Shall we fight or shall we fly?
     Good Sir Richard, tell us now,
     For to fight is but to die!
There'll be little of us left by the time this sun be set."
And Sir Richard said again: "We be all good Englishmen.
Let us bang these dogs of Seville, the children of the devil,
For I never turned my back upon Don or devil yet."

Sir Richard spoke and he laughed, and we roared a hurrah, and so
The little *Revenge* ran on sheer into the heart of the foe,
With her hundred fighters on deck, and her ninety sick below;
For half of their fleet to the right and half to the left were seen,
And the little *Revenge* ran on through the long sea-lane between.

Thousands of their soldiers looked down from their decks and laughed,
Thousands of their seamen made mock at the mad little craft
     Running on and on, till delayed
By their mountain-like *San Philip* that, of fifteen hundred tons,
And up-shadowing high above us with her yawning tiers of guns,
Took the breath from our sails, and we stayed.

And while now the great *San Philip* hung above us like a cloud,
     Whence the thunderbolt will fall
     Long and loud,
     Four galleons drew away
     From the Spanish fleet that day,
And two upon the larboard and two upon the starboard lay,
And the battle-thunder broke from them all.

But anon the great *San Philip*, she bethought herself and went,
Having that within her womb that had left her ill-content;
And the rest they came aboard us, and they fought us hand to hand,
For a dozen times they came with their pikes and musqueteers,
And a dozen times we shook 'em off as a dog that shakes his ears,
     When he leaps from the water to the land.

And the sun went down, and the stars came out far over the summer sea,
But never a moment ceased the fight of the one and fifty-three.
Ship after ship, the whole night long, their high-built galleons came,
Ship after ship, the whole night long, with her battle-thunder and flame;
Ship after ship, the whole night long, drew back with her dead and her shame,
For some were sunk and many were shattered, and so could fight us no more—
God of battles, was ever a battle like this in the world before?

     For he said "Fight on! fight on!"
     Tho' his vessel was all but a wreck;
And it chanced that, when half of the summer night was gone,
With a grisly wound to be drest, he had left the deck,
But a bullet struck him that was dressing it suddenly dead,
And himself, he was wounded again in the side and the head,
     And he said, "Fight on! fight on!"

And the night went down, and the sun smiled out far over the summer sea,
And the Spanish fleet with broken sides lay round us all in a ring;
But they dared not touch us again, for they feared that we still could sting,
    So they watched what the end would be.
    And we had not fought them in vain,
    But in perilous plight were we.
Seeing forty of our poor hundred were slain,
And half of the rest of us maim'd for life
In the crash of the cannonades and the desperate strife;
And the sick men down in the hold were most of them stark and cold,
And the pikes were all broken or bent, and the powder was all of it spent;
And the masts and the rigging were lying over the side;
But Sir Richard cried in his English pride,
"We have fought such a fight, for a day and a night,
As may never be fought again!
We have won great glory, my men!
    And a day less or more
    At sea or ashore,
    We die—does it matter when?
Sink me the ship, Master Gunner—sink her, split her in twain!
Fall into the hands of God, not into the hands of Spain!"

And the gunner said, "Ay, ay," but the seamen made reply:
    "We have children, we have wives,
    And the Lord hath spared our lives.
We will make the Spaniard promise, if we yield, to let us go;
We shall live to fight again and to strike another blow."
And the lion there lay dying, and they yielded to the foe.

And the stately Spanish men to their flagship bore him then,
Where they laid him by the mast, old Sir Richard caught at last,
And they praised him to his face with their courtly foreign grace;
But he rose upon their decks, and he cried:
"I have fought for Queen and Faith like a valiant man and true;
I have only done my duty as a man is bound to do:
With a joyful spirit I, Sir Richard Grenville, die!"
And he fell upon their decks, and he died.

And they stared at the dead that had been so valiant and true,
And had holden the power and glory of Spain so cheap
That he dared her with one little ship and his English few;
Was he devil or man? He was devil for aught they knew,
But they sank his body with honor down into the deep,
And they manned the *Revenge* with a swarthier, alien crew,
And away she sail'd with her loss and long'd for her own;
When a wind from the lands they had ruin'd awoke from sleep,
And the water began to heave and the weather to moan,
And or ever that evening ended, a great gale blew,
And a wave like the wave that is raised by an earthquake grew,
Till it smote on their hulls and their sails and their masts and their flags,
And the whole sea plunged and fell on the shot-shatter'd navy of Spain,
And the little *Revenge* herself went down by the island crags
    To be lost evermore in the main.

The Sally from Coventry [1642–1649]

WALTER THORNBURY

"Passion o' me!" cried Sir Richard Tyrone,
Spurring the sparks from the broad paving-stone,
"Better turn nurse and rock children to sleep,
Than yield to a rebel old Coventry Keep.
No, by my halidom, no one shall say,
Sir Richard Tyrone gave a city away."

Passion o' me! how he pulled at his beard,
Fretting and chafing if ony one sneered,
Clapping his breastplate and shaking his fist,
Giving his grizzly moustachios a twist,
Running the protocol through with his steel,
Grinding the letter to mud with his heel.

Then he roared out for a pottle of sack,
Clapped the old trumpeter twice on the back,
Leaped on his bay with a dash and a swing,
Bade all the bells in the city to ring,
And when the red flag from the steeple went down,
Open they flung every gate in the town.

To boot! and to horse! and away like a flood
A fire in their eyes, and a sting in their blood;
Hurrying out with a flash and a flare,
A roar of hot guns, a loud trumpeter's blare,
And first, sitting proud as a king on his throne,
At the head of them all dashed Sir Richard Tyrone.

Crimson and yellow, and purple and dun,
Fluttering scarf, flowing bright in the sun,
Steel like a mirror on brow and on breast,
Scarlet and white on their feather and crest,
Banner that blew in a torrent of red,
Borne by Sir Richard, who rode at their head.

The "trumpet" went down—with a gash on his poll,
Struck by the parters of body and soul.
Forty saddles were empty; the horses ran red
With foul Puritan blood from the slashes that bled.
Curses and cries and a gnashing of teeth,
A grapple and stab on the slippery heath,
And Sir Richard leaped up on the fool that went down,
Proud as a conqueror donning his crown.

They broke them a way through a flooding of fire,
Trampling the best blood of London to mire,
When suddenly rising a smoke and a blaze,
Made all "the dragon's sons" stare in amaze:
"O ho!" quoth Sir Richard, "my city grows hot,
I've left it rent paid to the villainous Scot."

The Battle of Naseby [1645]

By Obadiah Bind-Their-Kings-in-Chains-and-Their-
Nobles-with-Links-of-Iron, Sergeant in Ireton's Regiment

THOMAS BABINGTON MACAULAY

Oh! wherefore come ye forth in triumph from the north,
  With your hands, and your feet, and your raiment all red?
And wherefore doth your rout send forth a joyous shout?
  And whence be the grapes of the wine-press which ye tread?
Oh! evil was the root, and bitter was the fruit,
  And crimson was the juice of the vintage that we trod;
For we trampled on the throng of the haughty and the strong,
  Who sate in the high places and slew the saints of God.
It was about the noon of a glorious day of June,
  That we saw their banners dance and their cuirasses shine,
And the Man of Blood was there, with his long essenced hair,
  And Astley, and Sir Marmaduke, and Rupert of the Rhine.

Like a servant of the Lord, with his Bible and his sword,
  The general rode along us to form us to the fight;
When a murmuring sound broke out, and swelled into a shout
  Among the godless horsemen upon the tyrant's right.
And hark! like the roar of the billows on the shore,
  The cry of battle rises along their charging line:
For God! for the Cause! for the Church! for the Laws!
  For Charles, King of England, and Rupert of the Rhine!
The furious German comes, with his clarions and his drums,
  His bravoes of Alsatia and pages of Whitehall;
They are bursting on our flanks! Grasp your pikes! Close your ranks!
  For Rupert never comes but to conquer or to fall.

They are here—they rush on—we are broken—we are gone—
    Our left is borne before them like stubble on the blast.
O Lord, put forth thy might! O Lord, defend the right!
    Stand back to back, in God's name! and fight it to the last!
Stout Skippon hath a wound—the centre hath given ground.
    Hark! hark! what means the trampling of horsemen on our rear?
Whose banner do I see, boys? 'Tis he! thank God! 'tis he, boys!
    Bear up another minute! Brave Oliver is here!
 Their heads all stooping low, their points all in a row:
    Like a whirlwind on the trees, like a deluge on the dikes,
Our cuirassiers have burst on the ranks of the Accurst,
    And at a shock have scattered the forest of his pikes.

Fast, fast, the gallants ride, in some safe nook to hide
    Their coward heads, predestined to rot on Temple Bar;
And he—he turns! he flies! shame on those cruel eyes
    That bore to look on torture, and dare not look on war!
Ho, comrades! scour the plain; and ere ye strip the slain,
    First give another stab to make your search secure;
Then shake from sleeves and pockets their broad-pieces and lockets,
    The tokens of the wanton, the plunder of the poor.
Fools! your doublets shone with gold, and your hearts were gay and bold,
    When you kissed your lily hands to your lemans to-day;
And to-morrow shall the fox from her chambers in the rocks
    Lead forth her tawny cubs to howl above the prey.

Where be your tongues that late mocked at heaven, and hell, and fate?
    And the fingers that once were so busy with your blades?
Your perfumed satin clothes, your catches and your oaths?
    Your stage plays and your sonnets, your diamonds and your spades?
Down! down! for ever down, with the mitre and the crown!
    With the Belial of the court, and the Mammon of the Pope!
There is woe in Oxford halls, there is wail in Durham's stalls;
    The Jesuit smites his bosom, the bishop rends his cope.
And she of the seven hills shall mourn her children's ills,
    And tremble when she thinks on the edge of England's sword;
And the kings of earth in fear shall shudder when they hear
    What the hand of God hath wrought for the Houses and the Word!

Cavalier Tunes [1642–1649]

ROBERT BROWNING

I. Marching Along

Kentish Sir Byng stood for his King,
Bidding the crop-headed Parliament swing;
And, pressing a troop unable to stoop
And see the rogues flourish and honest folk droop,
Marched them along, fifty-score strong,
Great-hearted gentlemen, singing this song.

God for King Charles! Pym and such carles
To the Devil that prompts 'em their treasonous parles!
Cavaliers up! Lips from the cup,
Hands from the pasty, nor bite take nor sup
Till you're—
      Marching along, fifty-score strong,
      Great-hearted gentlemen, singing this song.

Hampden to Hell, and his obsequies' knell
Serve Hazelrig, Fiennes, and young Harry as well!
England, good cheer! Rupert is near!
Kentish and loyalists, keep we not here—
      Marching along, fifty-score strong,
      Great-hearted gentlemen, singing this song?

Then, God for King Charles! Pym and his snarls
To the Devil that pricks on such pestilent carles!
Hold by the right, you double your might;
So, onward to Nottingham, fresh for the fight,
      March we along, fifty-score strong,
      Great-hearted gentlemen, singing this song!

II. Give a Rouse

King Charles, and who'll do him right now?
King Charles, and who's ripe for fight now?
Give a rouse: here's, in Hell's despite now,
      King Charles!

Who gave me the goods that went since?
Who raised me the house that sank once?
Who helped me to gold I spent since?
Who found me in wine you drank once?
> *King Charles, and who'll do him right now?*
> *King Charles, and who's ripe for fight now?*
> *Give a rouse: here's, in Hell's despite now,*
> *King Charles!*

To whom used my boy George quaff else,
By the old fool's side that begot him?
For whom did he cheer and laugh else,
While Noll's damned troopers shot him?
> *King Charles, and who'll do him right now?*
> *King Charles, and who's ripe for fight now?*
> *Give a rouse: here's, in Hell's despite now,*
> *King Charles!*

III. Boot and Saddle

Boot, saddle, to horse, and away!
Rescue my Castle, before the hot day
Brightens to blue from its silvery grey,
> *Boot, saddle, to horse, and away!*

Ride past the suburbs, asleep as you'd say;
Many's the friend there, will listen and pray
"God's luck to gallants that strike up the lay—
> *Boot, saddle, to horse, and away!"*

Forty miles off, like a roebuck at bay,
Flouts Castle Brancepeth the Roundheads' array:
Who laughs, "Good fellows ere this, by my fay,
> *Boot, saddle, to horse, and away?"*

Who? My wife Gertrude; that, honest and gay,
Laughs when you talk of surrendering, "Nay!
I've better counsellors; what counsel they?
> *Boot, saddle, to horse, and away!"*

The Three Troopers [1653–1658]

WALTER THORNBURY

Into the Devil tavern
  Three booted troopers strode,
From spur to feather spotted and splashed
  With the mud of a winter road.
In each of their cups they dropped a crust,
  And stared at the guests with a frown;
Then drew their swords, and roared for a toast,
  "God send this Crum-well-down!"

A blue smoke rose from their pistol locks,
  Their sword blades were still wet;
There were long red smears on their jerkins of buff,
  As they the table overset.
Then into their cups they stirred the crusts,
  And cursed old London town;
They waved their swords, and drank with a stamp,
  "God send this Crum-well-down!"

The 'prentice dropped his can of beer.
  The host turned pale as a clout,
The ruby nose of the toping squires
  Grew white at the wild men's shout.
Then into their cups they flung their crusts,
  And shewed their teeth with a frown;
They flashed their swords as they gave the toast,
  "God send this Crum-well-down!"

The gambler dropped his dog's-ear'd cards,
  The waiting-women screamed,
As the light of the fire, like stains of blood,
  On the wild men's sabres gleamed.
Then into their cups they splashed their crusts,
  And cursed the fool of a town,
And leapt on the table, and roared a toast,
  "God send this Crum-well-down!"

Till on a sudden fire-bells rang,
    And the troopers sprang to horse;
The eldest muttered between his teeth,
    Hot curses—deep and coarse.
In their stirrup cups they flung the crusts,
    And cried as they spurred through the town,
With their keen swords drawn and their pistols cocked,
    "God send this Crum-well-down!"

Away they dashed through Temple Bar,
    Their red cloaks flowing free,
Their scabbards clashed, each back-piece shone—
    None like to touch the three.
The silver cups that held the crusts
    They flung to the startled town,
Shouting again, with a blaze of swords,
    "God send this Crum-well-down!"

The Song of the Western Men [1688]

R. S. HAWKER

A good sword and a trusty hand!
    A merry heart and true!
King James's men shall understand
    What Cornish lads can do.

And have they fixed the where and when?
    And shall Trelawney die?
Here's twenty thousand Cornish men
    Will know the reason why!

Out spake their captain brave and bold,
    A merry wight was he:
"If London Tower were Michael's hold
    We'll set Trelawney free!

"We'll cross the Tamar, land to land,
    The Severn is no stay,—
With one and all, and hand in hand,
    And who shall bid us nay?

"And when we come to London Wall,
    A pleasant sight to view,
Come forth! come forth, ye cowards all!
    Here's men as good as you.

"Trelawney he's in keep and hold
    Trelawney he may die;
But here's twenty thousand Cornish bold
    Will know the reason why!"

The British Grenadiers

ANONYMOUS

Some talk of Alexander, and some of Hercules;
Of Hector and Lysander, and such great names as these;
But of all the world's brave heroes, there's none that can compare,
With a tow, row, row, row, row, row, to the British Grenadier.

Those heroes of antiquity ne'er saw a cannon ball,
Or knew the force of powder to slay their foes withal;
But our brave boys do know it, and banish all their fears,
Sing tow, row, row, row, row, row, for the British Grenadiers.

Whene'er we are commanded to storm the palisades,
Our leaders march with fusees, and we with hand grenades;
We throw them from the glacis, about the enemies' ears,
Sing tow, row, row, row, row, row, for the British Grenadiers.

And when the siege is over, we to the town repair,
The townsmen cry Hurra, boys, here comes a Grenadier,
Here come the Grenadiers, my boys, who know no doubts or fears,
Then sing tow, row, row, row, row, row, for the British Grenadiers.

Then let us fill a bumper and drink a health to those
Who carry caps and pouches, and wear the louped clothes;
May they and their commanders live happy all their years,
With a tow, row, row, row, row, row, for the British Grenadiers.

The Battle of the Boyne [1690]

CAPTAIN BLACKER

July the first, in Oldbridge town, there was a grievous battle,
Where many a man lay on the ground by cannons that did rattle.
King James he pitched his tents between the lines for to retire;
But King William threw his bomb-balls in, and set them all on fire.

Thereat enraged they vowed revenge upon King William's forces,
And oft did vehemently cry that they would stop their courses.
A bullet from the Irish came and grazed King William's arm,
They thought his majesty was slain, yet it did him little harm.

Duke Schomberg then, in friendly care, his King would often caution
To shun the spot where bullets hot retained their rapid motion;
But William said, he don't deserve the name of Faith's defender,
Who would not venture life and limb to make a foe surrender.

When we the Boyne began to cross, the enemy they descended;
But few of our brave men were lost, so stoutly we defended;
The horse was the first that marched o'er, the foot soon followed after;
But brave Duke Schomberg was no more by venturing over the water.

When valiant Schomberg he was slain, King William did accost
His warlike men for to march on and he would be foremost;
"Brave boys," he said, "be not dismayed for the loss of one commander,
For God will be our king this day, and I'll be general under."

Then stoutly we the Boyne did cross, to give the enemies battle:
Our cannon, to our foe's great cost, like thundering claps did rattle.
In majestic mien our Prince rode o'er, his men soon followed after,
With blow and shout put our foes to the rout the day we crossed the water.

The Protestants of Drogheda have reason to be thankful,
That they were not to bondage brought, and tried at the Millmount after;
First to the Tholsel they were brought, and tried at the Millmount after;
But brave King William set them free by venturing over the water.

The cunning French near to Duleek had taken up their quarters,
And fenced themselves on every side, still waiting for new orders;
But in the dead time of the night, they set the fields on fire,
And long before the morning light, to Dublin they did retire.

Then said King William to his men, after the French departed,
"I'm glad" (said he) "that none of ye seem to be faint-hearted;
So sheath your swords and rest awhile, in time we'll follow after";
Those words he uttered with a smile the day he crossed the water.

Come let us all with heart and voice applaud our lives' defender,
Who at the Boyne his valor showed and made his foe surrender.
To God above the praise we'll give both now and ever after;
And bless the glorious memory of King William that crossed the water.

Rule, Britannia

JAMES THOMSON

When Britain first, at Heaven's command,
    Arose from out the azure main,
This was the charter of the land,
    And guardian angels sung this strain:
      "Rule, Britannia, rule the waves,
      Britons never will be slaves.

"The nations not so blessed as thee
    Must in their turn to tyrants fall;
While thou shalt flourish great and free,
    The dread and envy of them all.
      Rule, Britannia, rule the waves,
      Britons never will be slaves.

"Still more majestic shalt thou rise,
    More dreadful from each foreign stroke;
As the loud blast that tears the skies
    Serves but to root thy native oak.
      Rule, Britannia, rule the waves,
      Britons never will be slaves.

"Thee haughty tyrants ne'er shall tame:
    All their attempts to bend thee down
Will but arouse thy generous flame,
    But work their woe and thy renown.
      Rule, Britannia, rule the waves,
      Britons never will be slaves.

"To thee belongs the rural reign;
    Thy cities shall with commerce shine:
All thine shall be the subject main,—
    And every shore it circles, thine.
      Rule, Britannia, rule the waves,
      Britons never will be slaves.

"The Muses, still with freedom found,
    Shall to thy happy coast repair:
Blessed isle! with matchless beauty crowned,
    And manly hearts to guard the fair.
    Rule, Britannia, rule the waves,
    Britons never will be slaves."

ANONYMOUS

Neptune and Mars in Council sate
　　To humble France's pride,
Whose vain unbridled insolence
　　All other Powers defied.

The gods having sat in deep debate
　　Upon the puzzling theme,
Broke up perplexed and both agreed
　　Shirley should form the scheme.

Shirley, with Britain's glory fired,
　　Heaven's favoring smile implored:
"Let Louisburg return,"—he said,
　　"Unto its ancient Lord."

At once the Camp and Fleet were filled
　　With Britain's loyal sons,
Whose hearts are filled with generous strife
　　T' avenge their Country's wrongs.

With Liberty their breasts are filled.
　　Fair Liberty's their shield;
'Tis Liberty their banner waves
　　And hovers o'er their field.

Louis!—behold the unequal strife,
　　Thy slaves in walls immured!
While George's sons laugh at those walls—
　　Of victory assured.

One key to your oppressive pride
　　Your Western Dunkirk's gone;
So Pepperell and Warren bade
　　And what they bade was done!

Forbear, proud Prince, your gasconades,
　　Te Deums cease to sing,—
When Britons fight the *Grand Monarque*
　　Must yield to Britain's King.

Ode, Written in the Year 1746

WILLIAM COLLINS

How sleep the brave who sink to rest,
By all their country's wishes blest!
When Spring, with dewy fingers cold,
Returns to deck their hallowed mould,
She there shall dress a sweeter sod
Than Fancy's feet have ever trod.

By fairy hands their knell is rung,
By forms unseen their dirge is sung:
There Honor comes, a pilgrim gray,
To bless the turf that wraps their clay;
And Freedom shall awhile repair,
To dwell a weeping hermit there!

Battle of the Baltic [1801]

THOMAS CAMPBELL.

Of Nelson and the North
  Sing the glorious day's renown,
When to battle fierce came forth
  All the might of Denmark's crown,
And her arms along the deep proudly shone;
  By each gun the lighted brand
  In a bold, determined hand,
  And the Prince of all the land
      Led them on.

Like leviathans afloat
  Lay their bulwarks on the brine;
While the sign of battle flew
  On the lofty British line—
It was ten of April morn by the chime;
  As they drifted on their path
  There was silence deep as death,
  And the boldest held his breath
      For a time.

But the might of England flushed
  To anticipate the scene;
And her van the fleeter rushed
  O'er the deadly space between.—
"Hearts of oak!" our captain cried, when each gun
  From its adamantine lips
  Spread a death-shade round the ships,
  Like the hurricane eclipse
      Of the sun.

Again! again! again!
  And the havoc did not slack,
Till a feeble cheer the Dane
  To our cheering sent us back;
Their shots along the deep slowly boom:—
  Then ceased—and all is wail,
  As they strike the shattered sail,
  Or in conflagration pale,
      Light the gloom.

Out spoke the victor then,
  As he hailed them o'er the wave:
"Ye are brothers! ye are men!
  And we conquer but to save;—
So peace instead of death let us bring:
  But yield, proud foe, thy fleet,
  With the crews, at England's feet,
  And make submission meet
      To our King."

Then Denmark blessed our chief,
  That he gave her wounds repose;
And the sounds of joy and grief
  From her people wildly rose,
As death withdrew his shades from the day:
  While the sun looked smiling bright
  O'er a wide and woeful sight,
  Where the fires of funeral light
      Died away.

Now joy, old England, raise!
  For the tidings of thy might,
By the festal cities' blaze,
  Whilst the wine-cup shines in light;
And yet, amidst that joy and uproar,
  Let us think of them that sleep
  Full many a fathom deep,
  By thy wild and stormy steep,
      Elsinore!

Brave hearts! to Britain's pride
  Once so faithful and so true,
On the deck of fame that died,
  With the gallant, good Riou:—
Soft sigh the winds of heaven o'er their grave!
  While the billow mournful rolls,
  And the mermaid's song condoles,
  Singing glory to the souls
      Of the brave!

Ye Mariners of England

THOMAS CAMPBELL

Ye mariners of England,
That guard our native seas,
Whose flag has braved, a thousand years,
The battle and the breeze,
Your glorious standard launch again,
To match another foe!
And sweep through the deep
While the stormy winds do blow—
While the battle rages loud and long,
And the stormy winds do blow.

The spirits of your fathers
Shall start from every wave!
For the deck it was their field of fame,
And ocean was their grave.
Where Blake and mighty Nelson fell
Your manly hearts shall glow,
As ye sweep through the deep
While the stormy winds do blow—
While the battle rages loud and long,
And the stormy winds do blow.

Britannia needs no bulwarks,
No towers along the steep;
Her march is o'er the mountain-wave,
Her home is on the deep.
With thunders from her native oak
She quells the floods below,
As they roar on the shore
When the stormy winds do blow—
When the battle rages loud and long,
And the stormy winds do blow.

The meteor flag of England
Shall yet terrific burn,
Till danger's troubled night depart,
And the star of peace return.
Then, then, ye ocean-warriors!
Our song and feast shall flow
To the fame of your name,
When the storm has ceased to blow—
When the fiery fight is heard no more,
And the storm has ceased to blow.

The Burial of Sir John Moore at Corunna [1809]

CHARLES WOLFE

Not a drum was heard, not a funeral note,
    As his corse to the rampart we hurried;
Not a soldier discharged his farewell shot
    O'er the grave where our hero we buried.

We buried him darkly at dead of night,
    The sod with our bayonets turning;
By the struggling moonbeam's misty light,
    And the lantern dimly burning.

No useless coffin enclosed his breast,
    Not in sheet nor in shroud we wound him;
But he lay like a warrior taking his rest,
    With his martial cloak around him.

Few and short were the prayers we said,
    And we spoke not a word of sorrow;
But we steadfastly gazed on the face that was dead,
    And we bitterly thought of the morrow.

We thought, as we hollowed his narrow bed,
    And smoothed down his lonely pillow,
That the foe and the stranger would tread o'er his head,
    And we far away on the billow!

Lightly they'll talk of the spirit that's gone,
    And o'er his cold ashes upbraid him;
But little he'll reck if they let him sleep on,
    In the grave where a Briton has laid him.

But half of our heavy task was done,
    When the clock struck the hour for retiring;
And we heard the distant and random gun
    That the foe was sullenly firing.

Slowly and sadly we laid him down,
    From the field of his fame fresh and gory;
We carved not a line, and we raised not a stone—
    But we left him alone in his glory!

The Field of Waterloo [1815]

LORD BYRON

Stop! for thy tread is on an Empire's dust!
An Earthquake's spoil is sepulchred below!
Is the spot marked with no colossal bust?
Nor column trophied for triumphal show?
None; but the moral's truth tells simpler so,
As the ground was before, thus let it be;
How that red rain hath made the harvest grow!
And is this all the world has gained by thee,
Thou first and last of fields! king-making Victory?

There was a sound of revelry by night,
And Belgium's capital had gathered then
Her Beauty and her Chivalry, and bright
The lamps shone o'er fair women and brave men.
A thousand hearts beat happily; and when
Music arose with its voluptuous swell,
Soft eyes looked love to eyes which spake again
And all went merry as a marriage bell;
But hush! hark! a deep sound strikes like a rising knell!

Did ye not hear it?—No; 'twas but the wind,
Or the car rattling o'er the stony street;
On with the dance! let joy be unconfined;
No sleep till morn, when Youth and Pleasure meet
To chase the glowing Hours with flying feet.
But hark!—that heavy sound breaks in once more,
As if the clouds its echo would repeat;
And nearer, clearer, deadlier than before;
Arm! arm! it is—it is—the cannon's opening roar!

Within a windowed niche of that high hall
Sate Brunswick's fated chieftain; he did hear
That sound the first amidst the festival,
And caught its tone with Death's prophetic ear;
And when they smiled because he deemed it near,
His heart more truly knew that peal too well
Which stretched his father on a bloody bier,
And roused the vengeance blood alone could quell:
He rushed into the field, and, foremost fighting, fell.

Ah! then and there was hurrying to and fro,
And gathering tears, and tremblings of distress,
And cheeks all pale, which, but an hour ago,
Blushed at the praise of their own loveliness.
And there were sudden partings, such as press
The life from out young hearts, and choking sighs
Which ne'er might be repeated; who would guess
If ever more should meet those mutual eyes,
Since upon night so sweet such awful morn could rise!

And there was mounting in hot haste; the steed,
The mustering squadron, and the clattering car,
Went pouring forward with impetuous speed,
And swiftly forming in the ranks of war;
And the deep thunder, peal on peal afar:
And near, the beat of the alarming drum
Roused up the soldier ere the morning star;
While thronged the citizens with terror dumb,
Or whispering, with white lips—"The foe! they come! they come!"

And wild and high the "Cameron's gathering" rose!
The war-note of Lochiel, which Albyn's hills
Have heard, and heard, too, have her Saxon foes—
How in the noon of night that pibroch thrills,
Savage and shrill! but with the breath which fills
Their mountain-pipe, so fill the mountaineers
With the fierce native daring which instils
The stirring memory of a thousand years;
And Evan's, Donald's fame rings in each clansman's ears.

And Ardennes waves above them her green leaves,
Dewy with nature's tear drops, as they pass,
Grieving, if aught inanimate e'er grieves,
Over the unreturning brave—alas!
Ere evening to be trodden like the grass
Which now beneath them, but above shall grow
In its next verdure, when this fiery mass
Of living valor rolling on the foe,
And burning with high hope, shall moulder cold and low.

Last noon beheld them full of lusty life,
Last eve in Beauty's circle proudly gay;
The midnight brought the signal-sound of strife,
The morn the marshaling in arms,—the day
Battle's magnificently-stern array!
The thunder-clouds close o'er it, which, when rent,
The earth is covered thick with other clay,
Which her own clay shall cover, heaped and pent,
Rider and horse,—friend, foe,—in one red burial blent!

God Save the King

HENRY CAREY

God save our gracious King!
Long live our noble King!
    God save the King!
Send him victorious,
Happy and glorious,
Long to reign over us!
    God save the King!

O Lord our God, arise!
Scatter his enemies,
    And make them fall;
Confound their politics,
Frustrate their knavish tricks,
On Thee our hopes we fix—
    God save us all!

Thy choicest gifts in store
On him be pleased to pour;
    Long may he reign!
May he defend our laws,
And ever give us cause
To sing with heart and voice,
    God save the King!

The Lost Leader

ROBERT BROWNING

Just for a handful of silver he left us,
   Just for a riband to stick in his coat—
Found the one gift of which fortune bereft us,
   Lost all the others she lets us devote;
They, with the gold to give, doled him out silver,
   So much was theirs who so little allowed:
How all our copper had gone for his service!
   Rags—were they purple, his heart had been proud!
We that had loved him so, followed him, honored him,
   Lived in his mild and magnificent eye,
Learned his great language, caught his clear accents,
   Made him our pattern to live and to die!
Shakespeare was of us, Milton was for us,
   Burns, Shelley, were with us,—they watch from their graves!
He alone breaks from the van and the freemen,
   —He alone sinks to the rear and the slaves!

We shall march prospering,—not thro' his presence;
   Songs may inspirit us,—not from his lyre;
Deeds will be done,—while he boasts his quiescence,
   Still bidding crouch whom the rest bade aspire:
Blot out his name, then, record one lost soul more,
   One task more declined, one more footpath untrod,
One more devil's-triumph and sorrow for angels,
   One wrong more to man, one more insult to God!
Life's night begins: let him never come back to us!
   There would be doubt, hesitation and pain,
Forced praise on our part—the glimmer of twilight,
   Never glad confident morning again!
Best fight on well, for we taught him—strike gallantly
   Menace our heart ere we master his own;
Then let him receive the new knowledge and wait us,
   Pardoned in heaven, the first by the throne!

The Charge of the Heavy Brigade [1854]

ALFRED, LORD TENNYSON

The charge of the gallant Three Hundred, the Heavy Brigade
    Down the hill, down the hill, thousands of Russians,
Thousands of horsemen drew to the valley—and stayed.
    For Scarlett and Scarlett's Three Hundred were riding by
    When the points of the Russian lances broke in on the sky;
And he called "Left wheel into line!" and they wheeled and obeyed.
    Then he looked at the host that had halted, he knew not why,
And he turned half round, and he bade his trumpeter sound
    "To the charge!" and he rode on ahead, as he waved his blade
        To the gallant Three Hundred, whose glory will never die,
        "Follow and up the hill!"
Up the hill, up the hill followed the Heavy Brigade.

    The trumpet, the gallop, the charge, and the might of the fight!
        Down the hill, slowly, thousands of Russians
Drew to the valley, and halted at last on the height
With a wing pushed out to the left, and a wing to the right.
    But Scarlett was far on ahead, and he dashed up alone
        Through the great grey slope of men;
        And he whirled his sabre, he held his own
        Like an Englishman there and then.
And the three that were nearest him followed with force,
Wedged themselves in between horse and horse,
Fought for their lives in the narrow gap they had made,
    Four amid thousands; and up the hill, up the hill
Galloped the gallant Three Hundred, the Heavy Brigade.

            Fell, like a cannon-shot,
            Burst, like a thunderbolt,
            Crashed, like a hurricane
        Broke through the mass from below,
        Drove through the midst of the foe,
        Plunged up and down, to and fro,
        Rode flashing blow upon blow.
            Brave Inniskillings and Greys,

Whirling their sabres in circles of light,
And some of us all in amaze,
Who were held for a while from the fight
And were only standing at gaze,
When the dark-muffled Russian crowd
Folded its wings from the left and the right,
And rolled them around like a cloud—
Oh! mad for the charge and the battle were we
When our own good red coats sank from sight,
Like drops of blood in a dark gray sea;
And we turned to each other, muttering all dismayed:
"Lost are the gallant Three Hundred, the Heavy Brigade!"

But they rode, like victors and lords,
Through the forests of lances and swords;
In the heart of the Russian hordes
They rode, or they stood at bay;
Struck with the sword-hand and slew;
Down with the bridle-hand drew
The foe from the saddle and threw
Under foot there in the fray;
Ranged like a storm, or stood like a rock
In the wave of a stormy day;
Till suddenly shock upon shock
Staggered the mass from without;
For our men galloped up with a cheer and a shout,
And the Russians surged, and wavered and reeled
Up the hill, up the hill, up the hill, out of the field,
Over the brow and away.

Glory to each and to all, and the charge that they made!
Glory to all the Three Hundred, the Heavy Brigade!

The Charge of the Light Brigade [1854]

ALFRED, LORD TENNYSON

Half a league, half a league,
Half a league onward,
All in the valley of Death
    Rode the six hundred.
"Forward, the Light Brigade!
 Charge for the guns!" he said:
Into the valley of Death
    Rode the six hundred.

"Forward, the Light Brigade!"
Was there a man dismay'd?
Not tho' the soldier knew
    Some one had blundered.
Theirs not to make reply,
Theirs not to reason why,
Theirs but to do and die:
Into the Valley of Death
    Rode the six hundred.

Cannon to right of them,
Cannon to left of them,
Cannon in front of them
    Volley'd and thunder'd;
Storm'd at with shot and shell,
Boldly they rode and well:
Into the jaws of Death,
Into the mouth of Hell
    Rode the six hundred.

Flash'd all their sabres bare,
Flash'd as they turn'd in air
Sabring the gunners there,
Charging an army, while
    All the world wonder'd:
Plunged in the battery-smoke,
Right through the line they broke;
Cossack and Russian
Reel'd from the sabre-stroke
    Shatter'd and sunder'd.
Then they rode back, but not,
    Not the six hundred.

Cannon to right of them,
Cannon to left of them,
Cannon behind them
    Volley'd and thunder'd;
Storm'd at with shot and shell,
While horse and hero fell,
They that had fought so well
Came through the jaws of Death
Back from the mouth of Hell,
All that was left of them,
    Left of six hundred.

When can their glory fade?
O, the wild charge they made!
    All the world wonder'd.
Honor the charge they made!
Honor the Light Brigade,
    Noble six hundred!

The Last of the Light Brigade [1891]

RUDYARD KIPLING

There were thirty million English who talked of England's might,
There were twenty broken troopers who lacked a bed for the night.
They had neither food nor money, they had neither service nor trade;
They were only shiftless soldiers, the last of the Light Brigade.

They felt that life was fleeting; they knew not that art was long,
That though they were dying of famine, they lived in deathless song.
They asked for a little money to keep the wolf from the door;
And the thirty million English sent twenty pounds and four!

They had their heads together that were scarred and lined and grey;
Keen were the Russian sabres, but want was keener than they;
And an old Troop-Sergeant muttered, "Let us go to the man who writes
The things on Balaclava the kiddies at school recites."

They went without bands or colours, a regiment ten-file strong,
To look for the Master-singer who had crowned them all in his song;
And, waiting his servant's order, by the garden gate they stayed,
A desolate little cluster, the last of the Light Brigade.

They strove to stand to attention, to straighten the toil-bowed back;
They drilled on an empty stomach, the loose-knit files fell slack;
With stooping of weary shoulders, in garments tattered and frayed,
They shambled into his presence, the last of the Light Brigade.

The old Troop-Sergeant was spokesman, and "Beggin' your pardon," he said,
"You wrote o' the Light Brigade, sir. Here's all that isn't dead.
An' it's all come true what you wrote, sir, regardin' the mouth of hell;
For we're all of us nigh to the workhouse, an' we thought we'd call an' tell.

"No, thank you, we don't want food, sir; but couldn't you take an' write
A sort of 'to be continued' and 'see next page' o' the fight?
We think that someone has blundered, an' couldn't you tell 'em how?
You wrote we were heroes once, sir. Please, write we are starving now."

The poor little army departed, limping and lean and forlorn.
And the heart of the Master-singer grew hot with "the scorn of scorn."
And he wrote for them wonderful verses that swept the land like flame,
Till the fatted souls of the English were scourged with the thing called Shame.

O thirty million English that babble of England's might,
Behold there are twenty heroes who lack their food to-night;
Our children's children are lisping to "honour the charge they made—"
And we leave to the streets and the workhouse the charge of the Light Brigade!

The Song of the Camp

BAYARD TAYLOR

"Give us a song!" the soldiers cried,
  The outer trenches guarding,
When the heated guns of the camps allied
  Grew weary of bombarding.

The dark Redan, in silent scoff,
  Lay, grim and threatening, under;
And the tawny mound of the Malakoff
  No longer belched its thunder.

There was a pause. A guardsman said:
  "We storm the forts to-morrow;
Sing while we may, another day
  Will bring enough of sorrow."

They lay along the battery's side,
  Below the smoking cannon,—
Brave hearts from Severn and from Clyde
  And from the banks of Shannon.

They sang of love, and not of fame;
  Forgot was Britain's glory;
Each heart recalled a different name,
  But all sang *Annie Laurie.*

Voice after voice caught up the song
  Until its tender passion
Rose like an anthem, rich and strong.
  Their battle-eve confession.

Dear girl, her name he dared not speak
  But, as the song grew louder,
Something upon the soldier's cheek
  Washed off the stains of powder.

Beyond the darkening ocean burned
  The bloody sunset's embers,
While the Crimean valleys learned
  How English love remembers.

And once again a fire of hell
  Rained on the Russian quarters,
With scream of shot, and burst of shell,
  And bellowing of the mortars!

And Irish Nora's eyes are dim
  For a singer, dumb and gory;
And English Mary mourns for him
  Who sang of *Annie Laurie*.

Sleep, soldiers! still in honored rest
  Your truth and valor wearing;
The bravest are the tenderest,—
  The loving are the daring.

The Relief of Lucknow [1857]

ROBERT SPENCE LOWELL

Oh, that last day in Lucknow fort!
  We knew that it was the last;
That the enemy's mines crept surely in,
  And the end was coming fast.

To yield to that foe meant worse than death;
  And the men and we all worked on:
It was one day more of smoke and roar,
  And then it would all be done.

There was one of us, a corporal's wife,
  A fair, young, gentle thing,
Wasted with fever in the siege.
  And her mind was wandering.

She lay on the ground, in her Scottish plaid,
  And I took her head on my knee;
"When my father comes hame frae the pleugh," she said,
  "Oh! then please wauken me."

She slept like a child on father's floor,
  In the flecking of wood-bine shade,
When the house-dog sprawls by the open door,
  And the mother's wheel is stayed.

It was smoke and roar and powder-stench,
  And hopeless waiting for death;
And the soldier's wife, like a full-tired child,
  Seemed scarce to draw her breath.

I sank to sleep; and I had my dream
  Of an English village-lane,
And wall and garden; but one wild scream
  Brought me back to the roar again.

There Jessie Brown stood listening
  Till a sudden gladness broke
All over her face; and she caught my hand
  And drew me near and spoke:

"The Hielanders! Oh! dinna ye hear
  The slogan far awa?
The McGregor's? Oh! I ken it weel;
  It's the grandest o' them a'!

"God bless thae bonny Hielanders!
  We're saved! we're saved!" she cried;
And fell on her knees; and thanks to God
  Flowed forth like a full flood-tide.

Along the battery line her cry
  Had fallen among the men,
And they started back;—they were there to die;
  But was life so near them, then?

They listened for life; the rattling fire
  Far off, and the far-off roar,
Were all; and the colonel shook his head,
  And they turned to their guns once more.

Then Jessie said, "That slogan's done;
  But can ye hear them noo,
The Campbells are comin'? It's no a dream;
  Our succors hae broken through."

We heard the roar and the rattle afar,
  But the pipes we could not hear;
So the men plied their work of hopeless war,
  And knew that the end was near.

It was not long ere it made its way,
  A thrilling, ceaseless sound:
It was no noise from the strife afar,
  Or the sappers under ground.

It *was* the pipes of the Highlanders!
  And now they played *Auld Lang Syne.*
It came to our men like the voice of God,
  And they shouted along the line.

And they wept, and shook one another's hands,
  And the women sobbed in a crowd;
And every one knelt down where he stood,
  And we all thanked God aloud.

That happy day, when we welcomed them,
  Our men put Jessie first;
And the general gave her his hand, and cheers
  Like a storm from the soldiers burst.

And the pipers' ribbons and tartan streamed,
  Marching round and round our line;
And our joyful cheers were broken with tears,
  As the pipes played *Auld Lang Syne.*

1887

A. E. HOUSMAN

From Clee to heaven the beacon burns,
  The shires have seen it plain,
From north and south the sign returns
  And beacons burn again.

Look left, look right, the hills are bright,
  The dales are light between,
Because 'tis fifty years to-night
  That God has saved the Queen.

Now, when the flame they watch not towers
  About the soil they trod,
Lads, we'll remember friends of ours
  Who shared the work with God.

To skies that knit their heartstrings right,
  To fields that bred them brave,
The saviours come not home to-night:
  Themselves they could not save.

It dawns in Asia, tombstones show
  And Shropshire names are read;
And the Nile spills his overflow
  Beside the Severn's dead.

We pledge in peace by farm and town
  The Queen they served in war,
And fire the beacons up and down
  The land they perished for.

"God save the Queen" we living sing,
  From height to height 'tis heard;
And with the rest your voices ring,
  Lads of the Fifty-third.

Oh, God will save her, fear you not:
  Be you the men you've been,
Get you the sons your fathers got,
  And God will save the Queen.

Recessional

RUDYARD KIPLING

God of our fathers, known of old,
    Lord of our far-flung battle-line,
Beneath whose awful Hand we hold
    Dominion over palm and pine—
Lord God of Hosts, be with us yet,
Lest we forget—lest we forget!

The tumult and the shouting dies;
    The Captains and the Kings depart:
Still stands Thine ancient sacrifice,
    An humble and a contrite heart.
Lord God of Hosts, be with us yet,
Lest we forget—lest we forget!

Far-called, our navies melt away;
    On dune and headland sinks the fire:
Lo, all our pomp of yesterday
    Is one with Nineveh and Tyre!
Judge of the Nations, spare us yet,
Lest we forget—lest we forget!

If, drunk with sight of power, we loose
    Wild tongues that have not Thee in awe,
Such boastings as the Gentiles use,
    Or lesser breeds without the Law—
Lord God of Hosts, be with us yet,
Lest we forget—lest we forget!

For heathen heart that puts her trust
    In reeking tube and iron shard,
All valiant dust that builds on dust,
    And guarding, calls not Thee to guard,
For frantic boast and foolish word—
Thy mercy on Thy People, Lord!

The English Flag [1891]

RUDYARD KIPLING

Above the portico a flag-staff, bearing the Union
Jack, remained fluttering in the flames for some
time, but ultimately when it fell the crowds rent
the air with shouts, and seemed to see significance
in the incident.   —Daily Papers

Winds of the World, give answer! They are whimpering to and fro—
And what should they know of England who only England know?—
The poor little street-bred people that vapour and fume and brag,
They are lifting their heads in the stillness to yelp at the English Flag!

Must we borrow a clout from the Boer—to plaster anew with dirt?
An Irish liar's bandage, or an English coward's shirt?
We may not speak of England; her Flag's to sell or share.
What is the Flag of England? Winds of the World, declare!

The North Wind blew:—"From Bergen my steel-shod vanguards go;
I chase your lazy whalers home from the Disko floe.
By the great North Lights above me I work the will of God,
And the liner splits on the ice-field or the Dogger fills with cod.

"I barred my gates with iron, I shuttered my doors with flame,
Because to force my ramparts your nutshell navies came.
I took the sun from their presence, I cut them down with my blast,
And they died, but the Flag of England blew free ere the spirit passed.

"The lean white bear hath seen it in the long, long Arctic nights,
The musk-ox knows the standard that flouts the Northern Lights:
What is the Flag of England? Ye have but my bergs to dare,
Ye have but my drifts to conquer. Go forth, for it is there!"

The South Wind sighed:—"From the Virgins my mid-sea course was ta'en
Over a thousand islands lost in an idle main,
Where the sea-egg flames on the coral and the long-backed breakers croon
Their endless ocean legends to the lazy, locked lagoon.

"Strayed amid lonely islets, mazed amid outer keys,
  I waked the palms to laughter—I tossed the scud in the breeze.
  Never was isle so little, never was sea so lone,
  But over the scud and the palm-tree an English flag was flown.

"I have wrenched it free from the halliards to hand for a wisp on the Horn;
  I have chased it north to the Lizard—ribboned and rolled and torn;
  I have spread its folds o'er the dying, adrift in a hopeless sea;
  I have hurled it swift on the slaver, and seen the slave set free.

"My basking sunfish know it, and wheeling albatross,
  Where the lone wave fills with fire beneath the Southern Cross.
  What is the Flag of England? Ye have but my reefs to dare.
  Ye have but my seas to furrow. Go forth, for it is there!"

The East Wind roared:—"From the Kuriles, the Bitter Seas, I come,
And me men call the Home-Wind, for I bring the English home.
Look—look well to your shipping! By the breath of my mad typhoon
I swept your close-packed Praya and beached your best at Kowloon!

"The reeling junks behind me and the racing seas before,
  I raped your richest roadstead—I plundered Singapore!
  I set my hand on the Hoogli; as a hooded snake she rose;
  And I flung your stoutest steamers to roost with the startled crows.

"Never the lotos closes, never the wild-fowl wake,
  But a soul goes out on the East Wind that died for England's sake—
  Man or woman or suckling, mother or bride or maid—
  Because on the bones of the English the English Flag is stayed.

"The desert-dust hath dimmed it, the flying wild-ass knows,
  The scared white leopard winds it across the taintless snows.
  What is the Flag of England? Ye have but my sun to dare,
  Ye have but my sands to travel. Go forth, for it is there!"

The West Wind called:— "In squadrons the thoughtless galleons fly
That bear the wheat and cattle lest street-bred people die.
They make my might their porter, they make my house their path,
Till I loose my neck from their rudder and whelm them all in my wrath.

"I draw the gliding fog-bank as a snake is drawn from the hole.
They bellow one to the other, the frighted ship-bells toll;
For day is a drifting terror till I raise the shroud with my breath,
And they see strange bows above them and the two go locked to death.

"But whether in calm or wrack-wreath, whether by dark or day,
I heave them whole to the conger or rip their plates away,
First of the scattered legions, under a shrieking sky,
Dipping between the rollers, the English Flag goes by.

"The dead dumb fog hath wrapped it—the frozen dews have kissed—
The naked stars have seen it, a fellow-star in the mist.
What is the Flag of England? Ye have but my breath to dare,
Ye have but my waves to conquer. Go forth, for it is there!"

"Fuzzy-Wuzzy" [1896]

RUDYARD KIPLING

We've fought with many men acrost the seas,
   An' some of 'em was brave an' some was not:
The Paythan an' the Zulu an' Burmese;
   But the Fuzzy was the finest o' the lot.
We never got a ha'porth's change of 'im:
   'E squatted in the scrub an' 'ocked our 'orses,
'E cut our sentries up at Sua*kim*,
   An' 'e played the cat an' banjo with our forces.
     So 'ere's *to* you, Fuzzy-Wuzzy, at your 'ome in the Soudan;
     You're a pore benighted 'eathen but a first-class fightin' man;
     We gives you your certificate, an' if you want it signed
     We'll come an' 'ave a romp with you whenever you're inclined.

We took our chanst among the Kyber 'ills,
   The Boers knocked us silly at a mile,
The Burman give us Irriwaddy chills,
   An' a Zulu *impi* dished us up in style:
But all we ever got from such as they
   Was pop to what the Fuzzy made us swaller;
We 'eld our bloomin' own, the papers say,
   But man for man the Fuzzy knocked us 'oller.
     Then 'ere's *to* you, Fuzzy-Wuzzy, an' the missis and the kid;
     Our orders was to break you, an' of course we went an' did.
     We sloshed you with Martinis, an' it wasn't 'ardly fair;
     But for all the odds agin' you, Fuzzy-Wuz, you broke the square.

'E 'asn't got no papers of 'is own,
   'E 'asn't got no medals nor rewards,
So *we* must certify the skill 'e's shown
   In usin' of 'is long two-'anded swords:
When 'e's 'oppin' in an' out among the bush
   With 'is coffin-'eaded shield an' shovel-spear,
An 'appy day with Fuzzy on the rush
   Will last an 'ealthy Tommy for a year.
     So 'ere's *to* you, Fuzzy-Wuzzy, an' your friends which are no more,
     If we 'adn't lost some messmates we would 'elp you to deplore.
     But give an' take's the gospel, an' we'll call the bargain fair,
     For if you 'ave lost more than us, you crumpled up the square!

'E rushes at the smoke when we let drive,
    An', before we know, 'e's 'ackin' at our 'ead;
'E's all 'ot sand an' ginger when alive,
    An' 'e's generally shammin' when 'e's dead.
'E's a daisy, 'e's a ducky, 'e's a lamb!
    'E's a injia-rubber idiot on the spree,
'E's the on'y thing that doesn't give a damn
    For a Regiment o' British Infantree!
        So 'ere's *to* you, Fuzzy-Wuzzy, at your 'ome in the Soudan;
        You're a pore benighted 'eathen but a first-class fightin' man;
        An' 'ere's *to* you, Fuzzy-Wuzzy, with your 'ayrick 'ead of 'air—
        You big black boundin' beggar—for you broke a British square!

Sussex

RUDYARD KIPLING

God gave all men all earth to love,
    But, since our hearts are small,
Ordained for each one spot should prove
    Belovèd over all:
That, as He watched Creation's birth,
    So we, in godlike mood,
May of our love create our earth
    And see that it is good.

So one shall Baltic pines content,
    As one some Surrey glade,
Or one the palm-grove's droned lament
    Before Levuka's Trade.
Each to his choice, and I rejoice
    The lot has fallen to me
In a fair ground—in a fair ground—
    Yea, Sussex by the sea!

No tender-hearted garden crowns,
    No bosomed woods adorn
Our blunt, bow-headed, whale-backed Downs,
    But gnarled and writhen thorn—
Bare slopes where chasing shadows skim,
    And, through the gaps revealed,
Belt upon belt, the wooded, dim,
    Blue goodness of the Weald.

Clean of officious fence or hedge,
    Half-wild and wholly tame,
The wise turf cloaks the white cliff-edge
    As when the Romans came.
What sign of those that fought and died
    At shift of sword and sword?
The barrow and the camp abide,
    The sunlight and the sward.

Here leaps ashore the full Sou'west
    All heavy-winged with brine,
Here lies above the folded crest
    The Channel's leaden line;
And here the sea-fogs lap and cling,
    And here, each warning each,
The sheep-bells and the ship-bells ring
    Along the hidden beach.

We have no waters to delight
    Our broad and brookless vales—
Only the dewpond on the height
    Unfed, that never fails—
Whereby no tattered herbage tells
    Which way the season flies—
Only our close-bit thyme that smells
    Like dawn in Paradise.

Here through the strong and shadeless days
    The tinkling silence thrills;
Or little, lost, Down churches praise
    The Lord who made the hills:
But here the Old Gods guard their round,
    And, in her secret heart,
The heathen kingdom Wilfrid found
    Dreams, as she dwells, apart.

Though all the rest were all my share,
    With equal soul I'd see
Her nine-and-thirty sisters fair,
    Yet none more fair than she.
Choose ye your need from Thames to Tweed,
    And I will choose instead
Such lands as lie 'twixt Rake and Rye,
    Black Down and Beachy Head.

I will go out against the sun
　Where the rolled scarp retires,
And the Long Man of Wilmington
　Looks naked toward the shires;
And east till doubling Rother crawls
　To find the fickle tide,
By dry and sea-forgotten walls,
　Our ports of stranded pride.

I will go north about the shaws
　And the deep ghylls that breed
Huge oaks and old, the which we hold
　No more than Sussex weed;
Or south where windy Piddinghoe's
　Begilded dolphin veers,
And red beside wide-bankèd Ouse
　Lie down our Sussex steers.

So to the land our hearts we give
　Till the sure magic strike,
And Memory, Use, and Love make live
　Us and our fields alike—
That deeper than our speech and thought,
　Beyond our reason's sway,
Clay of the pit whence we were wrought
　Yearns to its fellow-clay.

God gives all men all earth to love,
　But, since man's heart is small,
Ordains for each one spot shall prove
　Belovèd over all.
Each to his choice, and I rejoice
　The lot has fallen to me
In a fair ground—in a fair ground—
　Yea, Sussex by the sea!

Peace [1914]

RUPERT BROOKE

Now, God be thanked Who has matched us with His hour,
   And caught our youth and wakened us from sleeping,
With hand made sure, clear eye, and sharpened power,
   To turn, as swimmers into cleanness leaping,
Glad from a world grown old and cold and weary,
   Leave the sick hearts that honour could not move,
And half-men, and their dirty songs and dreary,
   And all the little emptiness of love!

Oh! we, who have known shame, we have found release there,
   Where there's no ill, no grief, but sleep has mending,
     Naught broken save this body, lost but breath;
Nothing to shake the laughing heart's long peace there
   But only agony, and that has ending;
     And the worst friend and enemy is but Death.

The Soldier [1914]

RUPERT BROOKE

If I should die, think only this of me:
    That there's some corner of a foreign field
That is for ever England. There shall be
    In that rich earth a richer dust concealed;
A dust whom England bore, shaped, made aware,
    Gave once her flowers to love, her ways to roam,
A body of England's breathing English air,
    Washed by the rivers, blest by suns of home.

And think this heart, all evil shed away,
    A pulse in the eternal mind, no less
        Gives somewhere back the thoughts by England given;
Her sights and sounds: dreams happy as her day;
    And laughter, learnt of friends; and gentleness,
        In hearts at peace, under an English heaven.

Epitaph on an Army of Mercenaries [1914]

A. E. HOUSMAN

These, in the day when heaven was falling,
  The hour when earth's foundations fled,
Followed their mercenary calling
  And took their wages and are dead.

Their shoulders held the sky suspended;
  They stood, and earth's foundations stay;
What God abandoned, these defended,
  And saved the sum of things for pay.

A Wet Sheet and a Flowing Sea

ALLAN CUNNINGHAM

A wet sheet and a flowing sea,
A wind that follows fast,
And fills the white and rustling sail,
And bends the gallant mast;
And bends the gallant mast, my boys,
Awhile, like the eagle free,
Away the good ship flies, and leaves
Old England on the lee.

O for a soft and gentle wind!
I hear a fair one cry;
But give to me the snoring breeze,
And white waves heaving high;
And white waves heaving high, my boys,
The good ship tight and free—
The world of waters is our home,
And merry men are we.

There'e tempest in yon hornèd moon,
And lightning in yon cloud;
And hark the music, mariners!
The wind is piping loud;
The wind is piping loud, my boys,
The lightning flashing free—
While the hollow oak our palace is,
Our heritage the sea.

Gunga Din

RUDYARD KIPLING

You may talk o' gin and beer
When you're quartered safe out 'ere,
An' you're sent to penny-fights an' Aldershot it;
But when it comes to slaughter
You will do your work on water,
An' you'll lick the bloomin' boots of 'im that's got it.
Now in Injia's sunny clime,
Where I used to spend my time
A-servin' of 'Er Majesty the Queen,
Of all them blackfaced crew
The finest man I knew
Was our regimental bhisti, Gunga Din.
      He was "Din! Din! Din!
   You limpin' lump o' brick-dust, Gunga Din!
      Hi! Slippy *hitherao!*
      Water, get it! *Panee lao,*
   You squidgy-nosed old idol, Gunga Din."

The uniform 'e wore
Was nothin' much before,
An' rather less than 'arf o' that be'ind,
For a piece o' twisty rag
An' a goatskin water-bag
Was all the field-equipment 'e could find.
When the sweatin' troop-train lay
In a sidin' through the day,
Where the 'eat would make your bloomin' eyebrows crawl,
We shouted "Harry By!"
Till our throats were bricky-dry,
Then we wopped 'im 'cause 'e couldn't serve us all.
      It was "Din! Din! Din!
   You 'eathen, where the mischief 'ave you been?
      You put some *juldee* in it
      Or I'll *marrow* you this minute
   If you don't fill up my helmet, Gunga Din!"

'E would dot an' carry one
Till the longest day was done;
An' 'e didn't seem to know the use o' fear.
If we charged or broke or cut,
You could bet your bloomin' nut,
'E'd be waitin' fifty paces right flank rear.
With 'is mussick on 'is back,
'E would skip with our attack,
An' watch us till the bugles made "Retire,"
An' for all 'is dirty 'ide
'E was white, clear white, inside
When 'e went to tend the wounded under fire!
          It was "Din! Din! Din!"
    With the bullets kickin' dust-spots on the green.
          When the cartridges ran out,
          You could hear the front-ranks shout,
    "Hi! ammunition-mules an' Gunga Din!"

I shan't forgit the night
When I dropped be'ind the fight
With a bullet where my belt-plate should 'a' been.
I was chokin' mad with thirst,
An' the man that spied me first
Was our good old grinnin', gruntin' Gunga Din.
'E lifted up my 'ead,
An' he plugged me where I bled,
An' 'e guv me 'arf a pint o' water green
It was crawlin' and it stunk,
But of all the drinks I've drunk,
I'm gratefullest to one from Gunga Din.
          It was "Din! Din! Din!
    'Ere's a beggar with a bullet through 'is spleen;
          'E's chawin' up the ground;
          An' 'e's kickin' all around:
    For Gawd's sake git the water, Gunga Din!"

'E carried me away
To where a dooli lay,
An' a bullet come an' drilled the beggar clean.
'E put me safe inside,
An' just before 'e died,
"I 'ope you liked your drink," sez Gunga Din.
So I'll meet 'im later on
At the place where 'e is gone—
Where it's always double drill and no canteen.
'E'll be squattin' on the coals
Givin' drink to poor damned souls,
An' I'll get a swig in hell from Gunga Din!
       Yes, Din! Din! Din!
    You Lazarushian-leather Gunga Din!
       Though I've belted you and flayed you,
       By the livin' Gawd that made you,
    You're a better man than I am, Gunga Din!

Tommy

RUDYARD KIPLING

I went into a public-'ouse to get a pint o' beer,
The publican 'e up an' sez, "We serve no red-coats here."
The girls be'ind the bar they laughed an' giggled fit to die,
I outs into the street again an' to myself sez I:
　　O it's Tommy this, an' Tommy that, an' "Tommy, go away";
　　But it's "Thank you, Mister Atkins," when the band begins to play—
　　The band begins to play, my boys, the band begins to play,
　　O it's "Thank you, Mister Atkins," when the band begins to play.

I went into a theatre as sober as could be,
They gave a drunk civilian room, but 'asn't none for me;
They sent me to the gallery or round the music-'alls,
But when it comes to fightin', Lord! they'll shove me in the stalls!
　　For it's Tommy this, an' Tommy that, an' "Tommy, wait outside";
　　But it's "Special train for Atkins" when the trooper's on the tide—
　　The troopship's on the tide, my boys, the troopship's on the tide,
　　O it's "Special train for Atkins" when the trooper's on the tide.

Yes, makin' mock o' uniforms that guard you while you sleep
Is cheaper than them uniforms, an' they're starvation cheap;
An' hustlin' drunken soldiers when they're goin' large a bit
Is five times better business than paradin' in full kit.
　　Then it's Tommy this, an' Tommy that, an' "Tommy, 'ow's yer soul?"
　　But it's "Thin red line of 'eroes" when the drums begin to roll—
　　The drums begin to roll, my boys, the drums begin to roll,
　　O it's "Thin red line of 'eroes" when the drums begin to roll.

We aren't no thin red 'eroes, nor we aren't no blackguards too,
But single men in barricks, most remarkable like you;
An' if sometimes our conduck isn't all your fancy paints,
Why, single men in barricks don't grow into plaster saints;
　　While it's Tommy this, an' Tommy that, an' "Tommy, fall be'ind,"
　　But it's "Please to walk in front, sir," when there's trouble in the wind—
　　There's trouble in the wind, my boys, there's trouble in the wind,
　　O it's "Please to walk in front, sir," when there's trouble in the wind.

You talk o' better food for us, an' schools, an' fires, an' all:
We'll wait for extry rations if your treat us rational.
Don't mess about the cook-room slops, but prove it to our face
The Widow's Uniform is not the soldier-man's disgrace.
  For it's Tommy this, an' Tommy that, an' "Chuck him out, the brute!"
  But it's "Saviour of 'is country" when the guns begin to shoot;
  An' it's Tommy this, an' Tommy that, an' anything you please;
  An' Tommy ain't a bloomin' fool—you bet that Tommy sees!

Vitaï Lampada

SIR HENRY NEWBOLT

There's a breathless hush in the Close tonight—
Ten to make and the match to win—
A bumping pitch and a blinding light,
An hour to play and the last man in.
And it's not for the sake of a ribboned coat,
Or the selfish hope of a season's fame,
But his Captain's hand on his shoulder smote—
    "Play up! play up! and play the game!"

The sand of the desert is sodden red—
Red with the wreck of a square that broke;
The Gatling's jammed and the Colonel dead,
And the Regiment blind with dust and smoke.
The river of death has brimmed his banks,
And England's far and Honour a name,
But the voice of a schoolboy rallies the ranks:
    "Play up! play up! and play the game!"

This is the word that year by year,
While in her place the School is set,
Every one of her sons must hear,
And none that hears it dare forget.
This they all with a joyful mind
Bear through life like a torch in flame,
And falling fling to the host behind—
    "Play up! play up! and play the game!"

To an Athlete Dying Young

A. E. HOUSMAN

The time you won your town the race
We chaired you through the market-place;
Man and boy stood cheering by,
And home we brought you shoulder-high.

To-day, the road all runners come,
Shoulder-high we bring you home,
And set you at your threshold down,
Townsman of a stiller town.

Smart lad, to ship betimes away
From fields where glory does not stay
And early though the laurel grows
It withers quicker than the rose.

Eyes the shady night has shut
Cannot see the record cut,
And silence sounds no worse than cheers
After earth has stopped the ears:

Now you will not swell the rout
Of lads that wore their honours out,
Runners whom renown outran
And the name died before the man.

So set, before its echoes fade,
The fleet foot on the sill of shade,
And hold to the low lintel up
The still-defended challenge-cup.

And round that early-laurelled head
Will flock to gaze the strengthless dead,
And find unwithered on its curls
The garland briefer than a girl's.

Gentlemen-Rankers

RUDYARD KIPLING

To the legion of the lost ones, to the cohort of the damned,
  To my brethren in their sorrow overseas,
Sings a gentlemen of England cleanly bred, machinely crammed,
  And a trooper of the Empress, if you please.
Yes, a trooper of the forces who has run his own six horses,
  And faith he went the pace and went it blind,
And the world was more than kin while he held the ready tin,
  But to-day the Sergeant's something less than kind.

    We're poor little lambs who've lost our way,
        Baa! Baa! Baa!
    We're little black sheep who've gone astray,
        Baa—aa—aa!
    Gentlemen-rankers out on the spree,
    Damned from here to Eternity,
    God ha' mercy on such as we,
        Baa! Yah! Bah!

Oh, it's sweet to sweat through stables, sweet to empty kitchen slops,
  And it's sweet to hear the tales the troopers tell,
To dance with blowzy housemaids at the regimental hops
  And thrash the cad who says you waltz too well.
Yes, it makes you cock-a-hoop to be "Rider" to your troop,
  And branded with a blasted worsted spur,
When you envy O how keenly one poor Tommy living cleanly
  Who blacks your boots and sometimes calls you "Sir."

If the home we never write to, and the oaths we never keep,
  And all we know most distant and most dear
Across the snoring barrack-room return to break our sleep,
  Can you blame us if we soak ourselves in beer?
When the drunken comrade mutters and the great guard-lantern gutters
  And the horror of our fall is written plain,
Every secret, self-revealing on the aching whitewashed ceiling,
  Do you wonder that we drug ourselves from pain?

We have done with Hope and Honour, we are lost to Love and Truth,
    We are dropping down the ladder rung by rung,
And the measure of our torment is the measure of our youth.
    God help us, for we knew the worst too young!
Our shame is clean repentance for the crime that brought the sentence,
    Our pride it is to know no spur of pride,
And the Curse of Reuben holds us till an alien turf enfolds us
    And we die, and none can tell Them where we died.

        We're poor little lambs who've lost our way,
            Baa! Baa! Baa!
        We're little black sheep who've gone astray,
            Baa—aa—aa!
        Gentlemen-rankers out on the spree,
        Damned from here to Eternity,
        God ha' mercy on such as we,
            Baa! Yah! Bah!

Danny Deever

RUDYARD KIPLING

"What are the bugles flowin' for?" said Files-on-Parade.
"To turn you out, to turn you out," the Colour-Sergeant said.
"What makes you look so white, so white?" said Files-on-Parade.
"I'm dreadin' what I've got to watch," the Colour-Sergeant said.
   For they're hangin' Danny Deever, you can hear the Dead March play,
   The Regiment's in 'ollow square—they're hangin' him to-day;
   They've taken of his buttons off an' cut his stripes away,
   An' they're hangin' Danny Deever in the mornin'.

"What makes the rear-rank breathe so 'ard?" said Files-on-Parade.
"It's bitter cold, it's bitter cold," the Colour-Sergeant said.
"What makes that front-rank man fall down?" said Files-on-Parade.
"A touch o' sun, a touch o' sun," the Colour-Sergeant said.
   They are hangin' Danny Deever, they are marchin' of 'im round,
   They 'ave 'alted Danny Deever by 'is coffin on the ground;
   An' 'e'll swing in 'arf a minute for a sneakin' shootin' hound—
   O they're hangin' Danny Deever in the mornin'!

" 'Is cot was right-'and cot to mine," said Files-on-Parade.
" 'E's sleepin' out an' far to-night," the Colour-Sergeant said.
"I've drunk 'is beer a score o' times," said Files-on-Parade.
" 'E's drinkin'beer alone," the Colour-Sergeant said.
   They are hangin' Danny Deever, you must mark 'im to 'is place,
   For 'e shot a comrade sleepin'—you must look 'im in the face;
   Nine 'undred of 'is county an' the Regiment's disgrace,
   While they're hangin' Danny Deever in the mornin'.

"What's that so black agin the sun?" said Files-on-Parade.
"It's Danny fightin' 'ard for life," the Colour-Sergeant said.
"What's that that whimpers over'ead?" said Files-on-Parade.
"It's Danny's soul that's passin' now," the Colour-Sergeant said.
   For they're done with Danny Deever, you can 'ear the quickstep play,
   The Regiment's in column, an' they're marchin' us away;
   Ho! the young recruits are shakin', an' they'll want their beer to-day,
   After hangin Danny Deever in the mornin'!

SCOTLAND

This Is My Own, My Native Land

SIR WALTER SCOTT

Breathes there the man, with soul so dead,
Who never to himself hath said,
    This is my own, my native land!
Whose heart hath ne'er within him burn'd,
As home his footsteps he hath turn'd,
    From wandering on a foreign strand!
If such there breathe, go, mark him well;
For him no minstrel raptures swell;
High though his titles, proud his name,
Boundless his wealth as wish can claim:
Despite those titles, power, and pelf,
The wretch, concentred all in self,
Living, shall forfeit fair renown,
And, doubly dying, shall go down
To the vile dust, from whence he sprung,
Unwept, unhonor'd, and unsung.

O Caledonia! stern and wild,
Meet nurse for a poetic child!
Land of brown heath and shaggy wood,
Land of the mountain and the flood,
Land of my sires! what mortal hand
Can e'er untie the filial band,
That knits me to thy rugged strand!
Still, as I view each well-known scene,
Think what is now, and what hath been,
Seems as, to me, of all bereft,
Sole friends thy woods and streams were left;
And thus I love them better still,
Even in extremity of ill.
By Yarrow's streams still let me stray,
Though none should guide my feeble way;
Still feel the breeze down Ettrick break,
Although it chill my wither'd cheek;
Still lay my head by Teviot Stone,
Though there, forgotten and alone,
The Bard may draw his parting groan.

Bannockburn:

Robert Bruce's Address to His Army [1314]

ROBERT BURNS

Scots, wha hae wi' Wallace bled—
Scots, wham Bruce has aften led—
Welcome to your gory bed,
      Or to victorie!

Now's the day, and now's the hour;
See the front o' battle lower;
See approach proud Edward's power—
      Chains and slaverie!

Wha will be a traitor knave?
Wha can fill a coward's grave?
Wha sae base as be a slave?
      Let him turn and flee!

Wha for Scotland's king and law
Freedom's sword will strongly draw,
Freeman stand or freeman fa'—
      Let him follow me!

By oppression's woes and pains!
By your sons in servile chains!
We will drain our dearest veins,
      But they shall be free!

Lay the proud usurpers low!
Tyrants fall in every foe!
Liberty's in every blow!
      Let us do, or die!

The Battle of Otterbourne [1388]

ANONYMOUS

It fell about the Lammas tide,
  When the muir-men win their hay,
The doughty Douglas bound him to ride
  Into England to drive a prey.

He chose the Gordons and the Graemes
  With them the Lindsays light and gay;
But the Jardines wad not with him ride,
  And they rue it to this day.

And he has burned the dales o' Tyne,
  And part o' Bambrough shire,
And three good towers on Reidswire fells,
  And left them a' on fire.

And he marched up to Newcastel
  And rade it round about:
"O wha's the lord of this castel
  Or wha's the lady o 't?"

But up spake proud Lord Percy then,
  And O but he spake hie!
"I am the lord of this castel,
  My wife's the lady gay."

"If thou 'rt the lord of this castel,
  Sae weel it pleases me!
For, ere I cross the Border fells,
  The tane of us shall dee."—

He took a lang spear in his hand,
  Shod with the metal free;
And for to meet the Douglas there
  He rade richt furiouslie.

But O how pale his lady lookd
  Frae aff the castel wa',
As doun before the Scottish spear
  She saw proud Percy fa'!

"Had we twa been upon the green,
    And never an eye to see,
I wad hae had you, flesh and fell,
    But your sword sall gae wi' me.

"But gae ye up to Otterbourne,
    And bide there dayis three,
And gin I come not ere three dayis end,
    A fause knight ca' ye me!"

"The Otterbourne's a bonnie burn,
    'Tis pleasant there to be;
But there is nought at Otterbourne
    To feed my men and me.

"The deer rins wild on hill and dale,
    The birds fly wild frae tree to tree;
But there is neither bread nor kale,
    To fend my men and me.

"Yet I will stay at the Otterbourne,
    Where you shall welcome be;
And, if ye come not at three dayis end,
    A fause lord I'll ca' thee."

"Thither will I come," proud Percy said,
    "By the might of our Ladye!"
"There will I bide thee," said the Douglas,
    "My troth I plight to thee!"

They lichted high on Otterbourne,
    Upon the bent sae broun;
They lichted high on Otterbourne,
    And threw their pallions doun.

And he that had a bonnie boy,
    Sent out his horse to grass;
And he that had not a bonnie boy,
    His ain servant he was.

But up then spake a little page,
    Before the peep of dawn:
"O, waken ye, waken ye, my good lord,
    For Percy's hard at hand."

"Ye lee, ye lee, ye leear loud!
  Sae loud I hear ye lee:
For Percy had not men yestreen
  To dight my men and me.

"But I hae dreamed a dreary dream,
  Beyond the Isle o' Sky;
I saw a deid man win a fight,
  And I think that man was I."

He belted on his guid braidsword,
  And to the field he ran;
But he forgot the helmet good,
  That should have kept his brain.

When Percy wi' the Douglas met,
  I wot he was fu' fain:
They swakked their swords, till sair they swat,
  And the blude ran down like rain.

But Percy wi' his guid braidsword,
  That could sae sharply wound,
Has wounded Douglas on the brow,
  Till he fell to the ground.

And then he calld on his little foot-page,
  And said—"Run speedilie,
And fetch my ain dear sister's son,
  Sir Hugh Montgomery.

"My nephew guid!" the Douglas said.
  "What recks the death of ane?
Last night I dreamed a dreary dream,
  And I ken the day's thy ain!

"My wound is deep; I fain wad sleep!
  Tak' thou the vanguard o' the three,
And hide me by the bracken bush,
  That grows on yonder lilye lee.

"O bury me by the bracken bush,
  Beneath the blooming brier;
Let never living mortal ken
  That ere a kindly Scot lies here!"

He lifted up that noble lord,
  Wi' the saut tear in his ee;
And he hid him in the bracken bush,
  That his merrie men might not see.

The moon was clear, the day drew near,
  The spears in flinders flew;
But mony a gallant Englishman
  Ere day the Scotsmen slew.

The Gordons good, in English blude
  They steepd their hose and shoon;
The Lindsays flew like fire about,
  Till a' the fray was done.

The Percy and Montgomery met,
  That either of other was fain;
They swapped swords, and they twa swat,
  And aye the blude ran doun between.

"Now yield thee, yield thee, Percy!" he said,
  "Or else I vow I'll lay thee low!"
"To whom maun I yield," quoth Earl Percy,
  "Now that I see it maun be so?"

"Thou shalt not yield to lord nor loun,
  Nor yet shalt thou yield to me;
But yield thee to the bracken-bush
  That grows upon yan lilye lee!"

"I will not yield to a bracken-bush
  Nor yet will I yield to a brier;
But I wad yield to Earl Douglas,
  Or Sir Hugh the Montgomery, if he were here."

As soon as he knew it was Montgomery
  He struck his sword's point in the gronde;
The Montgomery was a courteous knight,
  And quickly took him by the honde.

This deed was done at the Otterbourne
  About the breaking o' the day;
Earl Douglas was buried at the bracken-bush,
  And the Percy led captive away.

Gathering Song of Donald the Black [1431]

SIR WALTER SCOTT

Pibroch of Donuil Dhu, pibroch of Donuil,
Wake thy wild voice anew, summon Clan-Conuil.
Come away, come away, hark to the summons!
Come in your war array, gentles and commons.

Come from deep glen, and from mountain so rocky,
The war-pipe and pennon are at Inverlochy.
Come every hill-plaid, and true heart that wears one,
Come every steel blade, and strong hand that bears one.

Leave untended the herd, the flock without shelter;
Leave the corpse uninterred, the bride at the altar;
Leave the deer, leave the steer, leave nets and barges:
Come with your fighting gear, broadswords and targes.

Come as the winds come, when forests are rended;
Come as the waves come, when navies are stranded:
Faster come, faster come, faster and faster,
Chief, vassal, page, and groom, tenant and master.

Fast they come, fast they come; see how they gather!
Wide waves the eagle plume, blended with heather.
Cast your plaids, draw your blades, forward each man set!
Pibroch of Donuil Dhu, knell for the onset!

JANE ELLIOTT

I've heard them lilting,
    At our yews' milking,—
Lasses a' lilting afore break of day;
    But now there's a moaning
    On ilka green loaning
The Flowers of the Forest are a' wede away.
    At the bughts, in the morning,
    Nae blithe lads are scorning;
The lasses are lonely, and dowie, and wae:
    Nae daffing, nae gabbing,
    But sighing and sabbing,
Ilk lass takes her leglin, and hies her away.

    At e'en in the gloaming,
    Nae swankies are roaming.
'Bout stacks wi' the lasses, at bogle to play;
    But ilk ane sits dreary,
    Lamenting her deary,—
The Flowers of the Forest are a' wede away.
    In har'st, at the shearing.
    Nae younkers are jeering,
The bandsters are runkled, lieard, and gray;
    At fair and at preaching,
    Nae wooing, nae fleeching,
The Flowers of the Forest are a' wede away.

    O dool for the order,
    Sent them to the border,
The English for anes by guile got the day;
    The Flowers of the Forest,
    That aye shone the fairest,
The prime of our land lies cauld in the clay.
    And now there's a moaning,
    On ilka green loaning,
The women and bairns are dowie and wae;
    There'll be nae mair lilting,
    At our yews' milking,
The Flowers of the Forest are a' wede away.

The Execution of Montrose [1650]

WILLIAM EDMONSTOUNE AYTOUN

Come hither, Evan Cameron,
    Come, stand beside my knee—
I hear the river roaring down
    Towards the wintry sea.
There's shouting on the mountain-side,
    There's war within the blast—
Old faces look upon me,
    Old forms go trooping past;
I hear the pibroch wailing
    Amidst the din of fight,
And my dim spirit wakes again
    Upon the verge of night.

'Twas I that led the Highland host
    Through wild Lochaber's snows,
What time the plaided clans came down
    To battle with Montrose.
I've told thee how the Southrons fell
    Beneath the broad claymore,
And how we smote the Campbell clan,
    By Inverlochy's shore.
I've told thee how we swept Dundee,
    And tamed the Lindsays' pride;
But never have I told thee yet
    How the great Marquis died.

A traitor sold him to his foes;
    O deed of deathless shame!
I charge thee, boy, if e'er thou meet
    With one of Assynt's name—
Be it upon the mountain's side,
    Or yet within the glen,
Stand he in martial gear alone,
    Or backed by armèd men—
Face him as thou wouldst face the man
    Who wronged thy sire's renown;
Remember of what blood thou art,
    And strike the caitiff down!

They brought him to the Watergate,
   Hard bound with hempen span,
As though they held a lion there,
   And not a fenceless man.
They set him high upon a cart—
   The hangman rode below—
They drew his hands behind his back,
   And bared his noble brow.
Then, as a hound is slipped from leash,
   They cheered, the common throng,
And blew the note with yell and shout,
   And bade him pass along.

It would have made a brave man's heart
   Grow sad and sick that day,
To watch the keen, malignant eyes
   Bent down on that array.
There stood the Whig west-country lords,
   In balcony and bow;
There sat the gaunt and withered dames,
   And their daughters all a-row.
And every open window
   Was full as full might be
With black-robed covenanting carles,
   That goodly sport to see!

But when he came, though pale and wan,
   He looked so great and high,
So noble was his manly front,
   So calm his steadfast eye;—
The rabble rout forebore to shout,
   And each man held his breath,
For well they knew the hero's soul
   Was face to face with death.
And then a mournful shudder
   Through all the people crept,
And some that came to scoff at him
   Now turned aside and wept.

But onwards—always onwards,
  In silence and in gloom,
The dreary pageant labored,
  Till it reached the house of doom.
Then first a woman's voice was heard
  In jeer and laughter loud,
And an angry cry and a hiss arose
  From the heart of the tossing crowd:
Then as the Graeme looked upwards,
  He saw the ugly smile
Of him who sold his king for gold—
  The master-fiend Argyle!

The Marquis gazed a moment,
  And nothing did he say,
But the cheek of Argyle grew ghastly pale
  And he turned his eyes away.
The painted harlot by his side,
  She shook through every limb,
For a roar like thunder swept the street,
  And hands were clenched at him;
And a Saxon soldier cried aloud,
  "Back, coward, from thy place!
For seven long years thou hast not dared
  To look him in the face."

Had I been there with sword in hand,
  And fifty Camerons by,
That day through high Dunedin's streets
  Had pealed the slogan-cry.
Not all their troops of trampling horse.
  Nor might of mailèd men—
Not all the rebels in the south
  Had borne us backwards then!
Once more his foot on highland heath
  Had trod as free as air,
Or I, and all who bore my name,
  Been laid around him there!

It might not be. They placed him next
  Within the solemn hall,
Where once the Scottish kings were throned
  Amidst their nobles all.
But there was dust of vulgar feet
  On that polluted floor,
And perjured traitors filled the place
  Where good men sate before.
With savage glee came Warristoun,
  To read the murderous doom;
And then uprose the great Montrose
  In the middle of the room.

"Now, by my faith, as belted knight,
  And by the name I bear,
And by the bright Saint Andrew's cross
  That waves above us there—
Yea, by a greater, mightier oath—
  And oh, that such should be!—
By that dark stream of royal blood
  That lies 'twixt you and me—
I have not sought in battle-field
  A wreath of such renown,
Nor dared I hope on my dying day
  To win the martyr's crown!

"There is a chamber far away
  Where sleep the good and brave,
But a better place ye have named for me
  Than by my father's grave.
For truth and right, 'gainst treason's might,
  This hand hath always striven,
And ye raise it up for a witness still
  In the eye of earth and heaven.
Then nail my head on yonder tower—
  Give every town a limb—
And God who made shall gather them:
  I go from you to Him!"

The morning dawned full darkly,
    The rain came flashing down,
And the jagged streak of the levin-bolt
    Lit up the gloomy town:
The thunder crashed across the heaven,
    The fatal hour was come;
Yet aye broke in with muffled beat,
    The 'larum of the drum.
There was madness on the earth below
    And anger in the sky,
And young and old, and rich and poor,
    Came forth to see him die.

Ah, God! that ghastly gibbet!
    How dismal 'tis to see
The great, tall, spectral skeleton,
    The ladder and the tree!
Hark! hark! it is the clash of arms—
    The bells begin to toll—
"He is coming! he is coming!—
    God's mercy on his soul!"
One last, long peal of thunder—
    The clouds are cleared away,
And the glorious sun once more looks down
    Amidst the dazzling day.

"He is coming! he is coming!"
    Like a bridegroom from his room
Came the hero from his prison
    To the scaffold and the doom.
There was glory on his forehead,
    There was lustre in his eye,
And he never walked to battle
    More proudly than to die;
There was color in his visage
    Though the cheeks of all were wan,
And they marveled as they saw him pass,
    That great and goodly man!

He mounted up the scaffold,
    And he turned him to the crowd;
But they dared not trust the people,
    So he might not speak aloud.
But he looked upon the heavens,
    And they were clear and blue,
And in the liquid ether
    The eye of God shone through.
Yet a black and murky battlement
    Lay resting on the hill,
As though the thunder slept within—
    All else was calm and still.

The grim Geneva ministers
    With anxious scowl drew near,
As you have seen the ravens flock
    Around the dying deer.
He would not deign them word nor sign,
    But alone he bent the knee;
And veiled his face for Christ's dear grace
    Beneath the gallows-tree.
Then radiant and serene he rose,
    And cast his cloak away:
For he had ta'en his latest look
    Of earth and sun and day.

A beam of light fell o'er him,
    Like a glory round the shriven,
And he climbed the lofty ladder
    As it were the path to heaven.
Then came a flash from out the cloud,
    And a stunning thunder-roll;
And no man dared to look aloft,
    For fear was on every soul.
There was another heavy sound,
    A hush and then a groan;
And darkness swept across the sky—
    The work of death was done!

The Bonnets o' Bonnie Dundee [1689]

SIR WALTER SCOTT

To the Lords o' Convention 'twas Claverhouse who spoke,
Ere the king's crown go down, there are crowns to be broke;
Then each cavalier who loves honor and me
Let him follow the bonnets o' bonnie Dundee!

Come fill up my cup, come fill up my can;
Come saddle my horses, and call out my men;
Come open the Westport and let us gae free,
And it's room for the bonnets o' bonnie Dundee!

Dundee he is mounted, he rides up the street,
The bells are rung backward, the drums they are beat;
But the provost, douce man, said, "Just e'en let him be,
The gude toun is weel rid o' that deil o' Dundee!"

As he rode doun the sanctified bends of the Bow,
Ilk carline was flyting and shaking her pow;
But the young plants o' grace they looked cowthie and slee,
Thinking, Luck to thy bonnet, thou bonnie Dundee!

With sour-featured whigs the Grass-Market was thranged,
As if half the west had set tryst to be hanged;
There was spite in each look, there was fear in each ee,
As they watched for the bonnets o' bonnie Dundee.

These cowls of Kilmarnock had spits and had spears,
And lang-hafted gullies to kill cavaliers;
But they shrunk to close-heads, and the causeway was free
At the toss o' the bonnet o' bonnie Dundee.

He spurred to the foot o' the proud castle rock,
And with the gay Gordon he gallantly spoke:
"Let Mons Meg and her marrows speak twa words or three,
For the love o' the bonnet o' bonnie Dundee."

The Gordon demands of him which way he goes.
"Where'er shall direct me the shade o' Montrose!
Your grace in short space shall hear tidings of me,
Or that low lies the bonnet o' bonnie Dundee.

"There are hills beyond Pentland and lands beyond Forth;
If there's lords in the lowland, there's chiefs in the north;
There are wild Duniewassals three thousand times three
Will cry 'Hey!' for the bonnet o' bonnie Dundee.

"There's brass on the target of barkened bull-hide,
There's steel in the scabbard that dangles beside;
The brass shall be burnished, the steel shall flash free,
At a toss o' the bonnet o' bonnie Dundee.

"Then awa' to the hills, to the lea, to the rocks,
Ere I own a usurper I'll couch with the fox:
And tremble, false whigs, in the midst o' your glee,
Ye hae no seen the last o' my bonnet and me."

He waved his proud hand, and the trumpets were blown,
The kettle-drums clashed, and the horsemen rode on,
Till on Ravelston's cliffs and on Clermiston's lea
Died away the wild war-notes o' bonnie Dundee.

Come fill up my cup, come fill up my can,
Come saddle the horses, and call up the men;
Come open your doors and let me gae free,
For it's up with the bonnets o' bonnie Dundee.

The Old Scottish Cavalier

WILLIAM EDMONSTOUNE AYTOUN

Come, listen to another song,
   Should make your heart beat high,
Bring crimson to your forehead,
   And the lustre to your eye;—
It is a song of olden time,
   Of days long since gone by,
And of a baron stout and bold
    As e'er wore sword on thigh!
      Like a brave old Scottish cavalier,
      All of the olden time!

He kept his castle in the North,
   Hard by the thundering Spey;
And a thousand vassals dwelt around,
   All of his kindred they.
And not a man of all that clan
   Had ever ceased to pray
For the Royal race they loved so well,
   Though exiled far away
      From the steadfast Scottish cavaliers
      All of the olden time!

His father drew the righteous sword
   For Scotland and her claims,
Among the loyal gentlemen
   And chiefs of ancient names,
Who swore to fight or fall beneath
   The standard of King James,
And died at Killiecrankie Pass,
   With the glory of the Graemes,
      Like a true old Scottish cavalier,
      All of the olden time!

He never owned the foreign rule,
   No master he obeyed;
But kept his clan in peace at home
   From foray and from raid;
And when they asked him for his oath,
   He touched his glittering blade,
And pointed to his bonnet blue,
   That bore the white cockade:
     Like a leal old Scottish cavalier,
     All of the olden time!

At length the news ran through the land,—
   The Prince had come again!
That night the fiery cross was sped
   O'er mountain and through glen;
And our old Baron rose in might,
   Like a lion from his den,
And rode away across the hills
   To Charlie and his men,
     With the valiant Scottish cavaliers,
     All of the olden time!

He was the first that bent the knee
   When the Standard waved abroad;
He was the first that charged the foe
   On Preston's bloody sod;
And ever in the van of fight
   The foremost still he trod.
Until on bleak Culloden's heath,
   He gave his soul to God,
     Like a good old Scottish cavalier,
     All of the olden time!

Oh! never shall we know again
   A heart so stout and true—
The olden times have passed away,
   And weary are the new:
The fair White Rose has faded
   From the garden where it grew,
And no fond tears, save those of heaven,
   The glorious bed bedew
     Of the last old Scottish cavalier,
     All of the olden time!

Wae's Me for Prince Charlie [1746]

WILLIAM GLEN

A wee bird cam' to our ha' door,
  He warbled sweet an' clearly,
An' aye the o'er-come o' his sang
  Was "Wae's me for Prince Charlie!"
Oh! when I heard the bonnie, bonnie bird,
  The tears cam' drappin' rarely,
I took my bannet aff my head,
  For weel I lo'ed Prince Charlie.

Quoth I, "My bird, my bonnie, bonnie bird,
  Is that a sang ye borrow,
Are these some words ye've learnt by heart,
  Or a lilt o' dool an' sorrow?"
"Oh! no, no, no," the wee bird sang,
  "I've flown sin' mornin' early,
But sic a day o' wind an' rain—
  Oh! wae's me for Prince Charlie!

"On hills that are, by right, his ain,
  He roves a lanely stranger,
On every side he's pressed by want,
  On every side is danger;
Yestreen I met him in a glen,
  My heart maist burstit fairly,
For sadly changed indeed was he—
  Oh! wae's me for Prince Charlie!

"Dark night cam' on, the tempest roared
  Loud o'er the hills an' valleys,
An' where was't that your Prince lay doun,
  Wha's hame should been a palace?
He rowed him in a Highland plaid,
  Which covered him but sparely,
An' slept beneath a bush o' broom—
  Oh! wae's me for Prince Charlie!"

But now the bird saw some redcoats,
  An' he shook his wings wi' anger,
"Oh! this is no a land for me;
  I'll tarry here nae langer!"
He hovered on the wing a while
  Ere he departed fairly,
But weel I mind the fareweel strain
  Was, "Wae's me for Prince Charlie!"

For A' That, and A' That

ROBERT BURNS

Is there, for honest poverty
  That hangs his head, and a' that?
The coward-slave, we pass him by;
  We dare be poor for a' that!
    For a' that, and a' that,
      Our toils obscure, and a' that:
    The rank is but the guinea's stamp,
      The man's the gowd for a' that!

What tho' on hamely fare we dine,
  Wear hodden-grey, and a' that?
Gie fools their silks, and knaves their wine,
  A man's a man for a' that!
    For a' that, and a' that,
      Their tinsel show, and a' that:
    The honest man, tho' e'er sae poor,
      Is king o' men for a' that!

Ye see yon birkie, ca'd a lord,
  Wha struts, and stares, and a' that:
Tho' hundreds worship at his word,
  He's but a coof for a' that:
    For a' that, and a' that,
      His riband, star, and a' that:
    The man of independent mind,
      He looks and laughs at a' that!

A prince can mak a belted knight,
  A marquis, duke, and a' that;
But an honest man's aboon his might:
  Guid faith, he mauna fa' that!
    For a' that, and a' that,
      Their dignities, and a' that,
    The pith o' sense, and pride o' worth
      Are higher rank than a' that.

Then let us pray that come it may—
    As come it will for a' that—
That sense and worth, o'er a' the earth,
    May bear the gree, and a' that:
      For a' that, and a' that,
        It's comin' yet for a' that,
      That man to man, the warld o'er,
        Shall brothers be for a' that!

My Heart's in the Highlands

ROBERT BURNS

My heart's in the Highlands, my heart is not here;
My heart's in the Highlands a-chasing the deer;
Chasing the wild deer, and following the roe,
My heart's in the Highlands wherever I go.
Farewell to the Highlands, farewell to the North,
The birthplace of valor, the country of worth;
Wherever I wander, wherever I rove,
The hills of the Highlands forever I love.

Farewell to the mountains high cover'd with snow;
Farewell to the straths and green valleys below;
Farewell to the forests and wild-hanging woods;
Farewell to the torrents and loud-pouring floods.
My heart's in the Highlands, my heart is not here;
My heart's in the Highlands a-chasing the deer;
Chasing the wild deer, and following the roe,
My heart's in the Highlands wherever I go.

The Campbells are Comin'

ANONYMOUS

The Campbells are comin', Oho, Oho,
The Campbells are comin', Oho, Oho,
The Campbells are comin' to bonnie Lochleven,
The Campbells are comin', Oho, Oho!

Upon the Lomonds, I lay, I lay,
Upon the Lomonds, I lay, I lay,
I lookit down to bonnie Lochleven,
And saw three bonnie perches play.
   The Campbells are comin', . . .

Great Argyle he goes before,
He makes his cannons and guns to roar;
Wi' sound o' trumpet, fife, and drum,
The Campbells are comin', Oho, Oho!
   The Campbells are comin', . . .

The Campbells they are a' wi' arms,
Their loyal faith and truth to show,
Wi' banners rattlin' in the wind
The Campbells are comin', Oho, Oho!
   The Campbells are comin,' . . .

Lochinvar

SIR WALTER SCOTT

O, young Lochinvar is come out of the west,
Through all the wide Border his steed was the best;
And save his good broadsword, he weapon had none,
He rode all unarmed, and he rode all alone.
So faithful in love, and so dauntless in war,
There never was knight like the young Lochinvar.

He staid not for brake, and he stopped not for stone,
He swam the Eske river where ford there was none;
But ere he alighted at Netherby gate,
The bride had consented, the gallant came late;
For a laggard in love, and a dastard in war,
Was to wed the Ellen of young Lochinvar.

So boldly he entered the Netherby Hall,
Among bridesmen and kinsmen, and brothers, and all:
Then spake the bride's father, his hand on his sword,
(For the poor craven bridegroom said never a word,)
"O come ye in peace here, or come ye in war,
Or to dance at our bridal, young Lord Lochinvar?"

"I long wooed your daughter, my suit you denied;
Love swells like the Solway, but ebbs like its tide—
And now am I come, with this lost love of mine,
To lead but one measure, drink one cup of wine.
There are maidens in Scotland more lovely by far,
That would gladly be bride to the young Lochinvar."

The bride kissed the goblet: the knight took it up,
He quaffed off the wine, and he threw down the cup.
She looked down to blush, and she looked up to sigh,
With a smile on her lips and a tear in her eye.
He took her soft hand, ere her mother could bar,—
"Now tread we a measure!" said young Lochinvar.

So stately his form, and so lovely her face,
That never a hall such a galliard did grace;
While her mother did fret, and her father did fume,
And the bridegroom stood dangling his bonnet and plume;
And the bride-maidens whispered, " 'T were better by far
To have matched our fair cousin with young Lochinvar."

One touch to her hand, and one word in her ear,
When they reached the hall-door, and the charger stood near;
So light to the croupe the fair lady he swung,
So light to the saddle before her he sprung.
"She is won! we are gone over bank, bush, and scaur;
They'll have fleet steeds that follow," quoth young Lochinvar.

There was mounting 'mong Graemes of the Netherby clan:
Forsters, Fenwicks, and Musgraves, they rode and they ran:
There was racing and chasing on Cannobie Lee,
But the lost bride of Netherby ne'er did they see.
So daring in love, and so dauntless in war,
Have ye e'er heard of gallant like young Lochinvar?

IRELAND

The Harp That Once through Tara's Halls

THOMAS MOORE

The harp that once through Tara's halls
    The soul of music shed,
Now hangs as mute on Tara's walls
    As if that soul were fled.
So sleeps the pride of former days,
    So glory's thrill is o'er,
And hearts that once beat high for praise
    Now feel that pulse no more.

No more to chiefs and ladies bright
    The harp of Tara swells:
The chord alone that breaks at night
    Its tale of ruin tells.
Thus Freedom now so seldom wakes,
    The only throb she gives
Is when some heart indignant breaks,
    To show that still she lives.

The Wearing of the Green [1798]

ANONYMOUS

O Paddy dear, and did you hear the news that's going round?
The shamrock is forbid by law to grow on Irish ground;
St. Patrick's day no more we'll keep, his colors can't be seen,
For there's a bloody law agin' the wearing of the green.
I met with Napper Tandy, and he took me by the hand,
And he said, "How's poor old Ireland, and how does she stand?"
She's the most distressful country that ever yet was seen,
They are hanging men and women there for wearing of the green.

Then since the color we must wear is England's cruel red,
Sure Ireland's sons will ne'er forget the blood that they have shed:
You may take the shamrock from your hat and cast it on the sod,
But 'twill take root and flourish still, though underfoot 'tis trod.
When the law can stop the blades of grass from growing as they grow,
And when the leaves in summer-time their color cease to show,
Then I will change the favor that I wear in my caubeen,
But till that day, please God, I'll stick to wearing of the green.

But if at last our color should be torn from Ireland's heart,
Her sons with shame and sorrow from the dear old soil will part;
I've heard whisper of a country that lies far beyond the sea,
Where rich and poor stand equal in the light of freedom's day:—
O Erin, must we leave you, driven by the tyrant's hand?
Must we ask a mother's blessing from a strange and distant land?
Where the cruel cross of England shall nevermore be seen,
And where, please God, we'll live and die still wearing of the green.

The Shan Van Vocht [1797]

ANONYMOUS

The sainted isle of old,
　Says the *shan van vocht;*
The parent and the mould
Of the beautiful and bold,
Has her sainted heart waxed cold?
　Says the *shan van vocht.*

Oh! the French are on the say,
　Says the *shan van vocht;*
Oh! the French are in the bay;
They'll be here without delay,
And the Orange will decay,
　Says the *shan van vocht.*
　　Oh! the French are in the bay,
　　They'll be here by break of day,
　　And the Orange will decay,
　　　Says the shan van vocht.

And their camp it shall be where?
　Says the *shan van vocht;*
Their camp it shall be where?
　Says the *shan van vocht.*
On the Currach of Kildare;
The boys they will be there
With their pikes in good repair,
　Says the *shan van vocht.*
　　To the Currach of Kildare
　　The boys they will repair,
　　And Lord Edward will be there,
　　　Says the shan van vocht.

Then what will the yeomen do?
   Says the *shan van vocht;*
What *will* the yeomen do?
   Says the *shan van vocht.*
What *should* the yeomen do,
But throw off the red and blue,
And swear that they'll be true
   To the *shan van vocht.*
     What should the yeomen do,
     But throw off the red and blue,
     And swear that they'll be true
      To the shan van vocht?

And what color will they wear?
   Says the *shan van vocht;*
What color will they wear?
   Says the *shan von vocht.*
What color *should* be seen,
Where our fathers' homes have been,
But our own immortal green?
   Says the *shan van vocht.*
     What color should be seen,
     Where our fathers' homes have been,
     But our own immortal green?
     Says the shan van vocht.

And will Ireland then be free?
   Says the *shan van vocht;*
Will Ireland then be free?
   Says the *shan van vocht;*
Yes! Ireland *shall* be free,
From the centre to the sea;
Then hurrah for liberty!
   Says the *shan van vocht.*
     Yes! Ireland shall *be free,*
     From the centre to the sea;
     Then hurrah for Liberty!
     Says the shan van vocht.

The Geraldines

THOMAS DAVIS

The Geraldines! the Geraldines!—'tis full a thousand years
Since, 'mid the Tuscan vineyards, bright flashed their battle-spears;
When Capet seized the crown of France, their iron shields were known,
And their sabre dint struck terror on the banks of the Garonne;
Across the downs of Hastings they spurred hard by William's side,
And the grey sands of Palestine with Moslem blood they dyed;
But never then, nor thence till now, have falsehood or disgrace
Been seen to soil Fitzgerald's plume, or mantle in his face.

The Geraldines! the Geraldines!—'tis true, in Strongbow's van,
By lawless force, as conquerors, their Irish reign began;
And, O! through many a dark campaign they proved their prowess stern,
In Leinster's plains, and Munster's vales, on king, and chief, and kerne:
But noble was the cheer within the halls so rudely won,
And generous was the steel-gloved hand that had such slaughter done!
How gay their laugh! how proud their mien! you'd ask no herald's sign—
Among a thousand you had known the princely Geraldine.

These Geraldines! these Geraldines!—not long our air they breathed,
Not long they fed on venison, in Irish water seethed,
Not often had their children been by Irish mothers nursed,
When from their full and genial hearts an Irish feeling burst!
The English monarchs strove in vain, by law, and force, and bribe,
To win from Irish thoughts and ways this "more than Irish" tribe;
For still they clung to fosterage, to Brehon, cloak, and bard:
What king dare say to Geraldine, "Your Irish wife discard?"

Ye Geraldines! ye Geraldines! how royally ye reigned
O'er Desmond broad and rich Kildare, and English arts disdained:
Your sword made knights, your banner waved, free was your bugle call
By Glyn's green slopes, and Dingle's tide, from Barrow's banks to Eochaill,
What gorgeous shrines, what Brehon lore, what minstrel feasts there were
In and around Magh Nuadhaid's keep, and palace-filled Adare!
But not for rite or feast ye stayed when friend or kin were pressed;
And foemen fled when "Crom abu" bespoke your lance in rest.

Ye Geraldines! ye Geraldines! since Silken Thomas flung
King Henry's sword on council board, the English thanes among,
Ye never ceased to battle brave against the English sway,
Though axe and brand and treachery your proudest cut away.
Of Desmond's blood through woman's veins passed on the exhausted tide;
His title lives—a Sassanach churl usurps the lion's hide;
And though Kildare tower haughtily, there's ruin at the root,
Else why, since Edward fell to earth, had such a tree no fruit?

True Geraldines! brave Geraldines! as torrents mould the earth,
You channeled deep old Ireland's heart by constancy and worth:
When Ginckle leaguered Limerick, the Irish soldiers gazed
To see if in the setting sun dead Desmond's banner blazed!
And still it is the peasants' hope upon the Curragh's mere,
"They live who'll see ten thousand men with good Lord Edward here."
So let them dream till brighter days, when, not by Edward's shade,
But by some leader true as he, their lines shall be arrayed!

These Geraldines! these Geraldines! rain wears away the rock,
And time may wear away the tribe that stood the battle's shock,
But ever, sure, while one is left of all that honored race,
In front of Ireland's chivalry is that Fitzgerald's place;
And though the last were dead and gone, how many a field and town,
From Thomas Court to Abbeyfeile, would cherish their renown!
And men will say of valor's rise, or ancient power's decline,
"'T will never soar, it never shone, as did the Geraldine."

The Geraldines! the Geraldines! and are there any fears
Within the sons of conquerors for full a thousand years?
Can treason spring from out a soil bedewed with martyrs' blood?
Or has that grown a purling brook which long rushed down a flood?
By Desmond swept with sword and fire, by clan and keep laid low,
By Silken Thomas and his kin, by sainted Edward! No!
The forms of centuries rise up, and in the Irish line
Command their sons to take the post that fits the Geraldine!

The Girl I Left Behind Me

ANONYMOUS

The dames of France are fond and free,
    And Flemish lips are willing,
And soft the maids of Italy,
    And Spanish eyes are thrilling;
Still, though I bask beneath their smile,
    Their charms fail to bind me,
And my heart falls back to Erin's Isle,
    To the girl I left behind me.

For she's as fair as Shannon's side,
    And purer than its water,
But she refus'd to be my bride
    Though many a year I sought her;
Yet, since to France I sail'd away,
    Her letters oft remind me,
That I promis'd never to gainsay
    The girl I left behind me.

She says, "My own dear love, come home,
    My friends are rich and many,
Or else, abroad with you I'll roam,
    A soldier stout as any;
If you'll not come, nor let me go,
    I'll think you have resign'd me,"—
My heart nigh broke when I answer'd "No,"
    To the girl I left behind me.

For never shall my true love brave
    A life of war and toiling,
And never as a skulking slave
    I'll tread my native soil on;
But, were it free or to be freed,
    The battle's close would find me
To Ireland bound, nor message need
    From the girl I left behind me.

OTHER LANDS

The Destruction of Sennacherib [c. 689 B.C.]

LORD BYRON

The Assyrian came down like a wolf on the fold,
And his cohorts were gleaming in purple and gold;
And the sheen of their spears was like stars on the sea,
When the blue wave rolls nightly on deep Galilee.

Like the leaves of the forest when Summer is green,
That host with their banners at sunset were seen;
Like the leaves of the forest when Autumn hath blown,
That host on the morrow lay withered and strown.

For the Angel of Death spread his wings on the blast,
And breathed in the face of the foe as he pass'd;
And the eyes of the sleepers wax'd deadly and chill,
And their hearts but once heaved, and for ever grew still!

And there lay the steed with his nostril all wide;
But through it there roll'd not the breath of his pride:
And the foam of his gasping lay white on the turf,
And cold as the spray of the rock-beating surf.

And there lay the rider, distorted and pale,
With the dew on his brow and the rust on his mail;
And the tents were all silent, the banners alone,
The lances uplifted, the trumpet unblown.

And the widows of Ashur are loud in their wail;
And the idols are broke in the temple of Baal;
And the might of the Gentile, unsmote by the sword,
Hath melted like snow in the glance of the Lord!

Horatius [363 B. C.]

THOMAS BABINGTON MACAULAY

Lars Porsena of Clusium
  By the Nine Gods he swore
That the great house of Tarquin
  Should suffer wrong no more.
By the Nine Gods he swore it,
  And named a trysting day,
And bade his messengers ride forth,
East and west and south and north,
  To summon his array.

East and west and south and north
  The messengers ride fast,
And tower and town and cottage
  Have heard the trumpet's blast.
Shame on the false Etruscan
  Who lingers in his home
When Porsena of Clusium
  Is on his march for Rome.

The horsemen and the footmen
  Are pouring in amain,
From many a stately market-place;
  From many a fruitful plain;
From many a lonely hamlet,
  Which, hid by beech and pine,
Like an eagle's nest, hangs on the crest
  Of purple Apennine;

From lordly Volaterrae,
  Where scowls the far-famed hold
Piled by the hands of giants
  For godlike kings of old;
From seagirt Populonia,
  Whose sentinels descry
Sardinia's snowy mountain tops
  Fringing the southern sky;

From the proud mart of Pisae,
    Queen of the western waves,
Where ride Massilia's triremes
    Heavy with fair-haired slaves;
From where sweet Clanis wanders
    Through corn and vines and flowers;
From where Cortona lifts to heaven
    Her diadem of towers.

Tall are the oaks whose acorns
    Drop in dark Auser's rill;
Fat are the stags that champ the boughs
Of the Ciminian hill,
Beyond all streams Clitumnus
    Is to the herdsman dear;
Best of all pools the fowler loves
    The great Volsinian mere.

But now no stroke of woodman
    Is heard by Auser's rill;
No hunter tracks the stag's green path
    Up the Ciminian hill;
Unwatched along Clitumnus
    Grazes the milk-white steer;
Unharmed the water fowl may dip
    In the Volsinian mere.

The harvests of Arretium,
    This year, old men shall reap;
This year, young boys in Umbro
    Shall plunge the struggling sheep;
And in the vats of Luna,
    This year, the must shall foam
Round the white feet of laughing girls
    Whose sires have marched to Rome.

There be thirty chosen prophets,
    The wisest of the land,
Who always by Lars Porsena
    Both morn and evening stand:
Evening and morn the Thirty
    Have turned the verses o'er,
Traced from the right on linen white
    By mighty seers of yore.

And with one voice the Thirty
    Have their glad answer given:
"Go forth, go forth, Lars Porsena;
    Go forth, beloved of Heaven;
Go, and return in glory
    To Clusium's royal dome;
And hang round Nurscia's altars
    The golden shields of Rome."

And now hath every city
    Sent up her tale of men;
The foot are fourscore thousand,
    The horse are thousands ten.
Before the gates of Sutrium
    Is met the great array.
A proud man was Lars Porsena
    Upon the trysting day.

For all the Etruscan armies
    Were ranged beneath his eye,
And many a banished Roman,
    And many a stout ally;
And with a mighty following
    To join the muster came
The Tusculan Mamilius,
    Prince of the Latian name.

But by the yellow Tiber
    Was tumult and affright:
From all the spacious champaign
    To Rome men took their flight.
A mile around the city,
    The throng stopped up the ways;
A fearful sight it was to see
    Through two long nights and days.

For aged folks on crutches,
    And women great with child,
And mothers sobbing over babes
    That clung to them and smiled,
And sick men borne in litters
    High on the necks of slaves,
And troops of sun-burned husbandmen
    With reaping-hooks and staves

And droves of mules and asses
 Laden with skins of wine,
And endless flocks of goats and sheep,
 And endless herds of kine,
And endless trains of wagons
 That creaked beneath the weight
Of corn-sacks and of household goods,
 Choked every roaring gate.

Now, from the rock Tarpeian,
 Could the wan burghers spy
The line of blazing villages
 Red in the midnight sky.
The Fathers of the City,
 They sat all night and day,
For every hour some horseman came
 With tidings of dismay.

To eastward and to westward
 Have spread the Tuscan bands;
Nor house, nor fence, nor dovecot
 In Crustumerium stands.
Verbenna down to Ostia
 Hath wasted all the plain;
Astur hath stormed Janiculum,
 And the stout guards are slain.

I wis, in all the Senate,
 There was no heart so bold,
But sore it ached, and fast it beat,
 When that ill news was told.
Forthwith up rose the Consul,
 Up rose the Fathers all;
In haste they girded up their gowns,
 And hied them to the wall.

They held a council standing
 Before the River-Gate;
Short time was there, ye well may guess,
 For musing or debate.
Out spake the Consul roundly:
 "The bridge must straight go down;
For, since Janiculum is lost,
 Nought else can save the town."

Just then a scout came flying,
  All wild with haste and fear:
"To arms! to arms! Sir Consul:
  Lars Porsena is here."
On the low hills to westward
  The Consul fixed his eye,
And saw the swarthy storm of dust
  Rise fast along the sky.

And nearer fast and nearer
  Doth the red whirlwind come;
And louder still and still more loud
From underneath that rolling cloud,
Is heard the trumpet's war-note proud,
  The trampling and the hum.
And plainly and more plainly
  Now through the gloom appears,
Far to left and far to right,
In broken gleams of dark-blue light,
The long array of helmets bright,
  The long array of spears.

And plainly and more plainly,
  Above that glimmering line,
Now might ye see the banners
  Of twelve fair cities shine;
But the banner of proud Clusium
  Was highest of them all,
The terror of the Umbrian,
  The terror of the Gaul.

And plainly and more plainly
  Now might the burghers know,
By port and vest, by horse and crest,
  Each warlike Lucumo.
There Cilnius of Arretium
  On his fleet roan was seen;
And Astur of the fourfold shield,
Girt with the brand none else may wield,
Tolumnius with the belt of gold,
And dark Verbenna from the hold
  By reedy Thrasymene.

Fast by the royal standard,
    O'erlooking all the war,
Lars Porsena of Clusium
    Sat in his ivory car.
By the right wheel rode Mamilius,
    Prince of the Latian name;
And by the left false Sextus,
    That wrought the deed of shame.

But when the face of Sextus
    Was seen among the foes,
A yell that rent the firmament
    From all the town arose.
On the house-tops was no woman
    But spat towards him and hissed,
No child but screamed out curses,
    And shook its little fist.

But the Consul's brow was sad,
    And the Consul's speech was low,
And darkly looked he at the wall,
    And darkly at the foe.
"Their van will be upon us
    Before the bridge goes down;
And if they once may win the bridge,
    What hope to save the town?"

Then out spake brave Horatius,
    The Captain of the Gate:
"To every man upon this earth
    Death cometh soom or late,
And how can man die better
    Than facing fearful odds,
For the ashes of his fathers,
    And the temples of his Gods,

"And for the tender mother
    Who dandled him to rest,
And for the wife who nurses
    His baby at her breast,
And for the holy maidens
    Who feed the eternal flame,
To save them from false Sextus
    That wrought the deed of shame?

"Hew down the bridge, Sir Consul,
    With all the speed ye may;
I, with two more to help me,
    Will hold the foe in play.
In yon strait path a thousand
    May well be stopped by three.
Now who will stand on either hand,
    And keep the bridge with me?"

Then out spake Spurius Lartius;
    A Ramnian proud was he:
"Lo, I will stand at thy right hand,
    And keep the bridge with thee."
And out spake strong Herminius;
    Of Titian blood was he:
"I will abide on thy left side,
    And keep the bridge with thee."

"Horatius," quoth the Consul,
    "As thou sayest, so let it be."
And straight against that great array
    Forth went the dauntless Three.
For Romans in Rome's quarrel
    Spared neither land nor gold,
Nor son nor wife, nor limb nor life,
    In the brave days of old.

Then none was for a party;
    Then all were for the state;
Then the great man helped the poor;
    And the poor man loved the great;
Then lands were fairly portioned;
    Then spoils were fairly sold;
The Romans were like brothers
    In the brave days of old.

Now Roman is to Roman
    More hateful than a foe,
And the Tribunes beard the high,
    And the Fathers grind the low.
As we wax hot in faction,
    In battle we wax cold;
Wherefore men fight not as they fought
    In the brave days of old.

Now while the Three were tightening
    Their harness on their backs,
The Consul was the foremost man
    To take in hand an axe;
And Fathers mixed with Commons,
    Seized hatchet, bar, and crow,
And smote upon the planks above,
    And loosed the props below.

Meanwhile the Tuscan army,
    Right glorious to behold,
Came flashing back the noonday light,
Rank behind rank, like surges bright
    Of a broad sea of gold.
Four hundred trumpets sounded
    A peal of warlike glee,
As that great host, with measured tread,
And spears advanced, and ensigns spread,
Rolled slowly towards the bridge's head,
    Where stood the dauntless Three.

The Three stood calm and silent,
    And looked upon the foes,
And a great shout of laughter
    From all the vanguard rose:
And forth three chiefs came spurring
    Before that deep array;
To earth they sprang, their swords they drew
And lifted high their shields, and flew
    To win the narrow way;

Aunus from green Tifernum,
    Lord of the Hill of Vines;
And Seius, whose eight hundred slaves
    Sicken in Ilva's mines;
And Picus, long to Clusium
    Vassal in peace and war,
Who led to fight his Umbrian powers
From that gray crag where, girt with towers,
The fortress of Nequinum lowers
    O'er the pale waves of Nar.

Stout Lartius hurled down Aunus
    Into the stream beneath:
Herminius struck at Seius,
    And clove him to the teeth:
At Picus brave Horatius
    Darted one fiery thrust;
And the proud Umbrian's gilded arms
    Clashed in the bloody dust.

Then Ocnus of Falerii
    Rushed on the Roman Three;
And Lausulus of Urgo,
    The Rover of the sea;
And Aruns of Volsinium
    Who slew the great wild boar,
The great wild boar that had his den
Amidst the reeds of Cosa's fen,
And wasted fields, and slaughtered men,
    Along Albinia's shore.

Herminius smote down Aruns:
    Lartius laid Ocnus low:
Right to the heart of Lausulus
    Horatius sent a blow.
"Lie there," he cried, "fell pirate!
    No more, aghast and pale,
From Ostia's walls the crowd shall mark
The track of thy destroying bark.
No more Campania's hinds shall fly
To woods and caverns when they spy
    Thy thrice accursed sail."

But now no sound of laughter
    Was heard among the foes.
A wild and wrathful clamor
    From all the vanguard rose.
Six spears' length from the entrance
    Halted that deep array,
And for a space no man came forth
    To win the narrow way.

But hark! the cry is Astur:
   And lo! the ranks divide;
And the great Lord of Luna
   Comes with his stately stride.
Upon his ample shoulders
   Clangs loud the fourfold shield,
And in his hand he shakes the brand
   Which none but he can wield.

He smiled on those bold Romans
   A smile serene and high;
He eyed the flinching Tuscans,
   And scorn was in his eye.
Quoth he: "The she-wolf's litter
   Stand savagely at bay;
But will ye dare to follow,
   If Astur clears the way?"

Then, whirling up his broadsword
   With both hands to the height,
He rushed against Horatius,
   And smote with all his might.
With shield and blade Horatius
   Right deftly turned the blow.
The blow, though turned, came yet too nigh;
It missed his helm, but gashed his thigh:
The Tuscans raised a joyful cry
   To see the red blood flow.

He reeled, and on Herminius
   He leaned one breathing-space;
Then, like a wild cat mad with wounds,
   Sprang right at Astur's face.
Through teeth, and skull, and helmet
   So fierce a thrust he sped,
The good sword stood a hand-breadth out
   Behind the Tuscan's head.

And the great Lord of Luna
   Fell at that deadly stroke
As falls on Mount Alvernus
   A thunder-smitten oak.
Far o'er the crashing forest
   The giant arms lie spread;
And the pale augurs, muttering low,
   Gaze on the blasted head.

On Astur's throat Horatius
   Right firmly pressed his heel,
And thrice and four times tugged amain
   Ere he wrenched out the steel.
"And see," he cried, "the welcome,
   Fair guests, that waits you here!
What Noble Lucumo comes next
   To taste our Roman cheer?"

But at his haughty challenge
   A sullen murmur ran,
Mingled of wrath, and shame, and dread,
   Along that glittering van.
There lacked not men of prowess,
   Nor men of lordly race;
For all Etruria's noblest
   Were round the fatal place.

But all Etruria's noblest
   Felt their hearts sink to see
On the earth the bloody corpses,
   In the path the dauntless Three:
And, from the ghastly entrance
   Where those bold Romans stood,
All shrank, like boys who unaware,
Ranging the woods to start a hare,
Come to the mouth of the dark lair
Where, growling low, a fierce old bear
   Lies amidst bones and blood.

Was none who would be foremost
　　To lead such dire attack:
But those behind cried "Forward!"
　　And those before cried "Back!"
And backward now and forward
　　Wavers the deep array;
And on the tossing sea of steel,
To and fro the standards reel;
And the victorious trumpet-peal
　　Dies fitfully away.

Yet one man for one moment
　　Stood out before the crowd;
Well known was he to all the Three,
　　And they gave him greeting loud:
"Now welcome, welcome Sextus!
　　Now welcome to thy home!
Why dost thou stay, and turn away?
Here lies the road to Rome."

Thrice looked he at the city;
　　Thrice looked he at the dead;
And thrice came on in fury,
　　And thrice turned back in dread:
And, white with fear and hatred,
　　Scowled at the narrow way
Where, wallowing in a pool of blood,
　　The bravest Tuscans lay.

But meanwhile axe and lever
　　Have manfully been plied;
And now the bridge hangs tottering
　　Above the boiling tide.
"Come back, come back, Horatius!"
　　Loud cried the Fathers all.
"Back, Lartius! back, Herminius!
　　Back, ere the ruin fall!"

Back darted Spurius Lartius;
  Herminius darted back:
And, as they passed, beneath their feet
  They felt the timbers crack.
But when they turned their faces,
  And on the farther shore
Saw brave Horatius stand alone,
  They would have crossed once more.

But with crash like thunder
  Fell every loosened beam,
And, like a dam, the mighty wreck
  Lay right athwart the stream:
And a long shout of triumph
  Rose from the walls of Rome,
As to the highest turret-tops
  Was splashed the yellow foam.

And, like a horse unbroken
  When first he feels the rein,
The furious river struggled hard,
  And tossed his tawny mane,
And burst the curb, and bounded,
  Rejoicing to be free,
And whirling down, in fierce career,
Battlement, and plank, and pier,
  Rushed headlong to the sea.

Alone stood brave Horatius,
  But constant still in mind;
Thrice thirty thousand foes before,
  And the broad flood behind.
"Down with him!" cried false Sextus,
  With a smile on his pale face.
"Now yield thee," cried Lars Porsena,
  "Now yield thee to our grace."

Round turned he, as not deigning
    Those craven ranks to see;
Nought spake he to Lars Porsena,
    To Sextus nought spake he;
But he saw on Palatinus
    The white porch of his home;
And he spake to the noble river
    That rolls by the towers of Rome

"O, Tiber! father Tiber!
    To whom the Romans pray,
A Roman's life, a Roman's arms,
    Take thou in charge this day!"
So he spake, and speaking sheathed
    The good sword by his side,
And with his harness on his back,
    Plunged headlong in the tide.

No sound of joy or sorrow
    Was heard from either bank:
But friends and foes in dumb surprise,
With parted lips and straining eyes,
    Stood gazing where he sank;
And when above the surges
    They saw his crest appear,
All Rome sent forth a rapturous cry,
And even the ranks of Tuscany
    Could scarce forbear to cheer.

But fiercely ran the current,
    Swollen high by months of rain;
And fast his blood was flowing;
    And he was sore in pain;
And heavy with his armor,
    And spent with changing blows:
And oft they thought him sinking,
    But still again he rose.

Never, I ween, did swimmer,
    In such an evil case,
Struggle through such a raging flood
    Safe to the landing place:
But his limbs were borne up bravely
    By the brave heart within,
And our good father Tiber
    Bore bravely up his chin.

"Curse on him!" quoth false Sextus;
    "Will not the villain drown?
But for this stay, ere close of day
    We should have sacked the town!"
"Heaven help him!" quoth Lars Porsena,
    "And bring him safe to shore;
For such a gallant feat of arms
    Was never seen before."

And now he feels the bottom;
    Now on dry earth he stands;
Now round him throng the Fathers
    To press his gory hands;
And now, with shouts and clapping,
    And noise of weeping loud,
He enters through the River-Gate,
    Borne by the joyous crowd.

They gave him of the corn-land,
    That was of public right,
As much as two strong oxen
    Could plough from morn till night;
And they made a molten image,
    And set it up on high,
And there it stands unto this day
    To witness if I lie.

It stands in the Comitium,
    Plain for all folk to see;
Horatius in his harness,
    Halting upon one knee:
And underneath is written,
    In letters all of gold,
How valiantly he kept the bridge
    In the brave days of old.

And still his name sounds stirring
  Unto the men of Rome,
As the trumpet-blast that cries to them
  To charge the Volscian home;
And wives still pray to Juno
  For boys with hearts as bold
As his who kept the bridge so well
  In the brave days of old.

And in the nights of winter,
  When the cold north winds blow,
And the long howling of the wolves
  Is heard amidst the snow;
When round the lonely cottage
  Roars loud the tempest's din,
And the good logs of Algidus
  Roar louder yet within;

When the oldest cask is opened,
  And the largest lamp is lit;
When the chestnuts glow in the embers,
  And the kid turns on the spit;
When young and old in circle
  Around the firebrands close;
When the girls are weaving baskets,
  And the lads are shaping bows;

When the goodman mends his armor,
  And trims his helmet's plume;
When the goodwife's shuttle merrily
  Goes flashing though the loom;
With weeping and with laughter
  Still is the story told,
How well Horatius kept the bridge
  In the brave days of old.

A Song to Mithras:

Hymn of the XXX Legion, *c.* A. D. 350

RUDYARD KIPLING

Mithras, God of the Morning, our trumpets waken the Wall!
"Rome is above the Nations, but Thou art over all!"
Now as the names are answered, and the guards are marched away,
Mithras, also a soldier, give us strength for the day!

Mithras, God of the Noontide, the heather swims in the heat.
Our helmets scorch our foreheads, our sandals burn our feet.
Now in the ungirt hour—now lest we blink and drowse,
Mithras, also a soldier, keep us true to our vows!

Mithras, God of the Sunset, low on the Western main—
Thou descending immortal, immortal to rise again!
Now when the watch is ended, now when the wine is drawn,
Mithras, also a soldier, keep us pure till the dawn!

Mithras, God of the Midnight, here where the great Bull dies,
Look on Thy children in darkness. Oh, take our sacrifice!
Many roads Thou hast fashioned—all of them lead to the Light!
Mithras, also a soldier, teach us to die aright!

Lepanto [1571]

G. K. CHESTERTON

White founts falling on the courts of the sun,
And the Soldan of Byzantium is smiling as they run;
There is laughter like the fountains in that face of all men feared,
It stirs the forest darkness, the darkness of his beard,
It curls the blood-red crescent, the crescent of his lips,
For the inmost sea of all the earth is shaken with his ships.
They have dared the white republics up the capes of Italy,
They have dashed the Adriatic round the Lion of the Sea,
And the Pope has cast his arms abroad for agony and loss,
And called the kings of Christendom for swords about the Cross.
The cold queen of England is looking in the glass;
The shadow of the Valois is yawning at the Mass;
From evening isles fantastical rings faint the Spanish gun,
And the Lord upon the Golden Horn is laughing in the sun.

Dim drums throbbing, in the hills half heard,
Where only on a nameless throne a crownless prince has stirred,
Where, risen from a doubtful seat and half-attainted stall,
The last knight of Europe takes weapons from the wall,
The last and lingering troubadour to whom the bird has sung,
That once went singing southward when all the world was young,
In that enormous silence, tiny and unafraid,
Comes up along a winding road the noise of the Crusade.
Strong gongs groaning as the guns boom far,
Don John of Austria is going to the war,
Stiff flags straining in the night-blasts cold
In the gloom black-purple, in the glint old-gold,
Torchlight crimson on the copper kettle-drums,
Then the tuckets, then the trumpets, then the cannon, and he comes.
Don John laughing in the brave beard curled,
Spurning of his stirrups like the thrones of all the world,
Holding his head up for a flag of all the free.
        Love-light of Spain—hurrah!
        Death-light of Africa!
        Don John of Austria
        Is riding to the sea.

Mahound is in his paradise above the evening star,
(*Don John of Austria is going to the war.*)
He moves a mighty turban on the timeless houri's knees,
His turban that is woven of the sunset and the seas.
He shakes the peacock gardens as he rises from his ease,
And he strides among the tree-tops and is taller than the trees,
And his voice through all the garden is a thunder sent to bring
Black Azrael and Ariel and Ammon on the wing.
        Giants and the Genii,
        Multiplex of wing and eye,
        Whose strong obedience broke the sky
        When Solomon was king.

They rush in red and purple from the red clouds of the morn,
From temples where the yellow gods shut up their eyes in scorn;
They rise in green robes roaring from the green hells of the sea
Where fallen skies and evil hues and eyeless creatures be;
On them the sea-valves cluster and the grey sea-forests curl,
Splashed with a splendid sickness, the sickness of the pearl;
They swell in sapphire smoke out of the blue cracks of the ground,—
They gather and they wonder and give worship to Mahound.
And he saith, "Break up the mountains where the hermit-folk may hide,
And sift the red and silver sands lest bone of saint abide,
And chase the Giaours flying night and day, not giving rest,
For that which was our trouble comes again out of the west.
We have set the seal of Solomon on all things under sun,
Of knowledge and of sorrow and endurance of things done,
But noise is in the mountains, in the mountains, and I know
The voice that shook our palaces—four hundred years ago:
It is he that saith not 'Kismet'; it is he that knows not Fate;
It is Richard, it is Raymond, it is Godfrey in the gate!
It is he whose loss is laughter when he counts the wager worth,
Put down your feet upon him, that our peace be on the earth."
For he heard drums groaning and he heard guns jar,
(*Don John of Austria is going to the war.*)
        Sudden and still—hurrah!
        Bolt from Iberia!
        Don John of Austria
        Is gone by Alcalar.

St. Michael's on his Mountain in the sea-roads of the north
(*Don John of Austria is girt and going forth.*)
Where the grey seas glitter and the sharp tides shift
And the sea folk labour and the red sails lift.
He shakes his lance of iron and he claps his wings of stone;
The noise is gone through Normandy; the noise is gone alone;
The North is full of tangled things and texts and aching eyes
And dead is all the innocence of anger and surprise,
And Christian killeth Christian in a narrow dusty room,
And Christian dreadeth Christ that hath a newer face of doom,
And Christian hateth Mary that God kissed in Galilee,
But Don John of Austria is riding to the sea.
Don John calling through the blast and the eclipse
Crying with the trumpet, with the trumpet of his lips,
        Trumpet that sayeth ha!
         Domino gloria!
        Don John of Austria
        Is shouting to the ships.

King Philip's in his closet with the Fleece about his neck
(*Don John of Austria is armed upon the deck.*)
The walls are hung with velvet that is black and soft as sin,
And little dwarfs creep out of it and little dwarfs creep in.
He holds a crystal phial that has colours like the moon,
He touches, and it tingles, and he trembles very soon,
And his face is as a fungus of a leprous white and grey
Like plants in the high houses that are shuttered from the day,
And death is in the phial, and the end of noble work,
But Don John of Austria has fired upon the Turk.
Don John's hunting, and his hounds have bayed—
Booms away past Italy the rumour of his raid.
        Gun upon gun, ha! ha!
        Gun upon gun, hurrah!
        Don John of Austria
        Has loosed the cannonade.

The Pope was in his chapel before day or battle broke,
(*Don John of Austria is hidden in the smoke.*)
The hidden room in a man's house where God sits all the year,
The secret window whence the world looks small and very dear.
He sees as in a mirror on the monstrous twilight sea
The crescent of his cruel ships whose name is mystery;
They fling great shadows foe-wards, making Cross and Castle dark,
They veil the plumed lions on the galleys of St. Mark;
And above the ships are palaces of brown, black-bearded chiefs,
And below the ships are prisons, where with multitudinous griefs,
Christian captives sick and sunless, all a labouring race repines
Like a race in sunken cities, like a nation in the mines.
They are lost like slaves that swat, and in the skies of morning hung
The stairways of the tallest gods when tyranny was young.
They are countless, voiceless, hopeless as those fallen or fleeing on
Before the high Kings' horses in the granite of Babylon.
And many a one grows witless in his quiet room in hell
Where a yellow face looks inward through the lattice of his cell,
And he finds his God forgotten, and he seeks no more a sign—
(*But Don John of Austria has burst the battle-line!*)
Don John pounding from the slaughter-painted poop,
Purpling all the ocean like a bloody pirate's sloop,
Scarlet running over on the silvers and the golds,
Breaking of the hatches up and bursting of the holds,
Thronging of the thousands up that labour under sea
White for bliss and blind for sun and stunned for liberty.
   Vivat Hispania!
   Domino Gloria!
   Don John of Austria
   Has set his people free!

Cervantes on his galley sets the sword back in the sheath
(*Don John of Austria rides homeward with a wreath.*)
And he sees across a weary land a straggling road in Spain,
Up which a lean and foolish knight forever rides in vain,
And he smiles, but not as Sultans smile, and settles back the blade. . . .
(*But Don John of Austria rides home from the Crusade.*)

Ivry [1590]

THOMAS BABINGTON MACAULAY

Now glory to the Lord of Hosts, from whom all glories are!
And glory to our Sovereign Liege, King Henry of Navarre!
Now let there be the merry sound of music and of dance,
Through thy corn-fields green, and sunny vines, O pleasant land of France!
And thou, Rochelle, our own Rochelle, proud city of the waters,
Again let rapture light the eyes of all thy mourning daughters.
As thou wert constant in our ills, be joyous in our joy,
For cold, and stiff, and still are they who wrought thy walls annoy.
Hurrah! hurrah! a single field hath turned the chance of war,
Hurrah! hurrah! for Ivry, and Henry of Navarre.

Oh! how our hearts were beating, when at the dawn of day,
We saw the army of the League drawn out in long array;
With all its priest-led citizens, and all its rebel peers,
And Appenzel's stout infantry, and Egmont's Flemish spears.
There rode the brood of false Lorraine, the curses of our land;
And dark Mayenne was in the midst, a truncheon in his hand:
And, as we looked on them, we thought of Seine's empurpled flood,
And good Coligni's hoary hair all dabbled with his blood;
And we cried unto the living God, who rules the fate of war,
To fight for our own holy name, and Henry of Navarre.

The King is come to marshal us, in all his armor drest,
And he has bound a snow-white plume upon his gallant crest.
He looked upon his people, and a tear was in his eye;
He looked upon the traitors, and his glance was stern and high.
Right graciously he smiled on us, as rolled from wing to wing,
Down all our line, a deafening shout, "God save our Lord the King!"
"And if my standard-bearer fall, as fall full well he may,
For never saw I promise yet of such a bloody fray,
Press where ye see my white plume shine, amidst the ranks of war,
And be your oriflamme to-day the helmet of Navarre."

Hurrah! the foes are moving. Hark to the mingled din
Of fife, and steed, and trump, and drum, and roaring culverin.
The fiery Duke is pricking fast across Saint André's plain,
With all the hireling chivalry of Guelders and Almayne.
Now by the lips of those ye love, fair gentlemen of France,
Charge for the golden lilies,—upon them with the lance.
A thousand spurs are striking deep, a thousand spears in rest,
A thousand knights are pressing close behind the snow-white crest;
And in they burst, and on they rushed, while, like a guiding star,
Amidst the thickest carnage blazed the helmet of Navarre.

Now, God be praised, the day is ours. Mayenne hath turned his rein.
D'Aumale hath cried for quarter. The Flemish count is slain.
Their ranks are breaking like thin clouds before a Biscay gale;
The field is heaped with bleeding steeds, and flags, and cloven mail.
And then we thought on vengeance, and, all along our van,
"Remember St. Bartholomew," was passed from man to man.
But out spake gentle Henry: "No Frenchman is my foe:
Down, down with every foreigner, but let your brethren go."
Oh! was there ever such a knight, in friendship or in war,
As our Sovereign Lord, King Henry, the soldier of Navarre?

Right well fought all the Frenchmen who fought for France to-day;
And many a lordly banner God gave them for a prey.
But we of the religion have borne us best in fight;
And the good Lord of Rosny hath ta'en the cornet white.
Our own true Maximilian the cornet white hath ta'en,
The cornet white with crosses black, the flag of false Lorraine.
Up with it high; unfurl it wide; that all the host may know
How God hath humbled the proud house which wrought his church such woe.
Then on the ground, while trumpets sound their loudest point of war,
Fling the red shreds, a footcloth neat for Henry of Navarre.

Ho! maidens of Vienna; Ho! matrons of Lucerne;
Weep, weep, and rend your hair for those who never shall return.
Ho! Philip, send, for charity, thy Mexican pistoles,
That Antwerp monks may sing a mass for thy poor spearmen's souls.
Ho! gallant nobles of the League, look that your arms be bright;
Ho! burghers of Saint Genevieve, keep watch and ward tonight.
For our God hath crushed the tyrant, our God hath raised the slave,
And mocked the counsel of the wise, and the valor of the brave.
Then glory to his holy name, from whom all glories are;
And glory to our Sovereign Lord, King Henry of Navarre.

How They Brought the Good News from Ghent to Aix

ROBERT BROWNING

I sprang to the stirrup, and Joris, and he;
I galloped, Dirck galloped, we galloped all three;
"Good speed!" cried the watch, as the gate-bolts undrew;
"Speed!" echoed the wall to us galloping through;
Behind shut the postern, the lights sank to rest,
And into the midnight we galloped abreast.

Not a word to each other; we kept the great pace
Neck by neck, stride by stride, never changing our place;
I turned in my saddle and made its girths tight,
Then shortened each stirrup, and set the pique right,
Rebuckled the cheek-strap, chained slacker the bit,
Nor galloped less steadily Roland a whit.

'Twas moonset at starting; but while we drew near
Lokeren, the cocks crew and twilight dawned clear;
At Boom, a great yellow star came out to see;
At Düffeld, 'twas morning as plain as could be;
And from Mechlen church-steeple we heard the half-chime,
So Joris broke silence with, "Yet there is time!"

At Aerschot, up leaped of a sudden the sun,
And against him the cattle stood black every one,
To stare thro' the mist at us galloping past,
And I saw my stout galloper Roland at last,
With resolute shoulders, each butting away
The haze, as some bluff river headland its spray,

And his low head and crest, just one sharp ear bent back
For my voice, and the other pricked out on his track;
And one eye's black intelligence,—ever that glance
O'er its white edge at me, his own master, askance!
And the thick heavy spume-flakes which aye and anon
His fierce lips shook upwards in galloping on.

By Hasselt, Dirck groaned; and cried Joris, "Stay spur!
Your Roos galloped bravely, the fault's not in her,
We'll remember at Aix"—for one heard the quick wheeze
Of her chest, saw the stretched neck and staggering knees,
And sunk tail, and horrible heave of the flank,
As down on her haunches she shuddered and sank.

So we were left galloping, Joris and I,
Past Looz and past Tongres, no cloud in the sky;
The broad sun above laughed a pitiless laugh,
'Neath our feet broke the brittle bright stubble like chaff;
Till over by Dalhem a dome-spire sprang white,
And "Gallop," gasped Joris, "for Aix is in sight!

"How they'll greet us!" and all in a moment his roan
Rolled neck and croup over, lay dead as a stone;
And there was my Roland to bear the whole weight
Of the news which alone could save Aix from her fate,
With his nostrils like pits full of blood to the brim,
And with circles of red for his eye-socket's rim.

Then I cast loose my buffcoat, each holster let fall,
Shook off both my jack-boots, let go belt and all,
Stood up in the stirrup, leaned, patted his ear,
Called my Roland his pet-name, my horse without peer;
Clapped my hands, laughed and sang, any noise, bad or good,
Till at length into Aix Roland galloped and stood.

And all I remember is, friends flocking round
As I sate with his head 'twixt my knees on the ground,
And no voice but was praising this Roland of mine,
As I poured down his throat our last measure of wine,
Which (the burgesses voted by common consent)
Was no more than his due who brought good news from Ghent.

The Battle of Hohenlinden [1800]

THOMAS CAMPBELL

On Linden, when the sun was low,
All bloodless lay the untrodden snow;
And dark as winter was the flow
    Of Iser, rolling rapidly.

But Linden saw another sight,
When the drum beat at dead of night,
Commanding fires of death to light
    The darkness of her scenery.

By torch and trumpet fast array'd,
Each horseman drew his battle-blade,
And furious every charger neigh'd,
    To join the dreadful revelry.

Then shook the hills with thunder riven,
Then rushed the steed to battle driven;
And louder than the bolts of heaven,
    Far flash'd the red artillery.

But redder yet that light shall glow,
On Linden's hills of stained snow;
And bloodier yet the torrent flow
    Of Iser, rolling rapidly.

'Tis morn; but scarce yon level sun,
Can pierce the war-clouds, rolling dun,
Where furious Frank and fiery Hun
    Shout in their sulph'rous canopy.

The combat deepens: On, ye brave!
Who rush to glory, or the grave!
Wave, Munich! all thy banners wave!
    And charge with all thy chivalry!

Few, few shall part where many meet!
The snow shall be their winding sheet,
And every turf beneath their feet
    Shall be a soldier's sepulchre!

The Isles of Greece

LORD BYRON

The isles of Greece, the isles of Greece!
  Where burning Sappho loved and sung,
Where grew the arts of war and peace,
  Where Delos rose, and Phoebus sprung!
Eternal summer gilds them yet,
But all, except their sun, is set.

The Scian and the Teian muse,
  The hero's harp, the lover's lute,
Have found the fame your shores refuse:
  Their place of birth alone is mute
To sounds which echo further west
Than your sires' "Islands of the Blest."

The mountains look on Marathon—
  And Marathon looks on the sea;
And musing there an hour alone,
  I dream'd that Greece might still be free;
For standing on the Persians' grave,
I could not deem myself a slave.

A king sate on the rocky brow
  Which looks o'er sea-born Salamis;
And ships by thousands, lay below,
  And men in nations;—all were his!
He counted them at break of day—
And when the sun set where were they?

And where are they? and where art thou,
  My country? On thy voiceless shore
The heroic lay is tuneless now—
  The heroic bosom beats no more!
And must thy lyre, so long divine,
Degenerate into hands like mine?

'Tis something, in the dearth of fame,
  Though link'd among a fetter'd race,
To feel at least a patriot's shame.
  Even as I sing, suffuse my face;
For what is left the poet here?
For Greeks a blush—for Greece a tear.

Must *we* but weep o'er days more blest?
  Must *we* but blush?—Our fathers bled.
Earth! render back from out thy breast
  A remnant of our Spartan dead!
Of the three hundred grant but three,
To make a new Thermopylae!

What, silent still? and silent all?
  Ah! no;—the voices of the dead
Sound like a distant torrent's fall,
  And answer, "Let one living head,
But one arise,—we come, we come!"
'Tis but the living who are dumb.

In vain—in vain: strike other chords;
  Fill high the cup with Samian wine!
Leave battles to the Turkish hordes,
  And shed the blood of Scio's vine!
Hark! rising to the ignoble call—
How answers each bold Bacchanal!

You have the Pyrrhic dance as yet;
  Where is the Pyrrhic phalanx gone?
Of two such lessons, why forget
  The nobler and the manlier one?
You have the letters Cadmus gave—
Think ye he meant them for a slave?

Fill high the bowl with Samian wine!
  We will not think of themes like these!
It made Anacreon's song divine:
  He served—but served Polycrates—
A tyrant; but our masters then
Were still, at least, our countrymen.

The tyrant of the Chersonese
    Was freedom's best and bravest friend;
That tyrant was Miltiades!
    Oh! that the present hour would lend
Another despot of the kind!
Such chains as his were sure to bind.

Fill high the bowl with Samian wine!
    On Suli's rock, and Parga's shore,
Exists the remnant of a line
    Such as the Doric mothers bore;
And there, perhaps, some seed is sown,
The Heracleidan blood might own.

Trust not for freedom to the Franks—
    They have a king who buys and sells;
In native swords, and native ranks.
    The only hope of courage dwells:
But Turkish force, and Latin fraud,
Would break your shield, however broad.

Fill high the bowl with Samian wine!
    Our virgins dance beneath the shade—
I see their glorious black eyes shine;
    But gazing on each glowing maid,
My own the burning tear-drop laves,
To think such breasts must suckle slaves.

Place me on Sunium's marbled steep,
    Where nothing, save the waves and I,
May hear our mutual murmurs sweep;
    There, swan-like, let me sing and die:
A land of slaves shall ne'er be mine—
Dash down yon cup of Samian wine!

Incident of the French Camp [1809]

ROBERT BROWNING

You know, we French stormed Ratisbon:
    A mile or so away
On a little mound, Napoleon
    Stood on our storming-day;
With neck out-thrust, you fancy how,
    Legs wide, arms locked behind.
As if to balance the prone brow
    Oppressive with its mind.

Just as perhaps he mused "My plans
    That soar, to earth may fall,
Let once my army-leader Lannes
    Waver at yonder wall,"—
Out 'twixt the battery-smokes there flew
    A rider, bound on bound
Full-galloping; nor bridle drew
    Until he reached the mound.

Then off there flung in smiling joy,
    And held himself erect
By just his horse's mane, a boy:
    You hardly could suspect—
(So tight he kept his lips compressed,
    Scarce any blood came through)
You looked twice ere you saw his breast
    Was all but shot in two.

"Well," cried he, "Emperor, by God's grace
    We've got you Ratisbon!
The Marshal's in the market-place,
    And you'll be there anon
To see your flag-bird flap his vans
    Where I, to heart's desire,
Perched him!" The Chief's eye flashed; his plans
    Soared up again like fire.

The Chief's eye flashed; but presently
  Softened itself, as sheathes
A film the mother-eagle's eye
  When her bruised eaglet breathes:
"You're wounded!" "Nay," his soldier's pride
  Touched to the quick, he said:
"I'm killed, Sire!" And his Chief beside,
  Smiling the boy fell dead.

The Ballad of East and West [1889]

RUDYARD KIPLING

Oh, East is East, and West is West, and never the twain shall meet,
Till Earth and Sky stand presently at God's great Judgment Seat,
But there is neither East nor West, Border, nor Breed, nor Birth,
  When two strong men stand face to face,
  though they come from the ends of the earth!

Kamal is out with twenty men to raise the Border-side,
And he has lifted the Colonel's mare that is the Colonel's pride.
He has lifted her out of the stable-door between the dawn and the day,
And turned the calkins upon her feet, and ridden her far away.
Then up and spoke the Colonel's son that led a troop of the Guides:
"Is there never a man of all my men can say where Kamal hides?"
Then up and spoke Mohammed Khan, the son of the Ressaldar,
"If ye know the track of the morning-mist, ye know where his pickets are.
At dusk he harries the Abazai—at dawn he is into Bonair,
But he must go by Fort Bukloh to his own place to fare.
So if ye gallop to Fort Bukloh as fast as a bird can fly,
By the favour of God ye may cut him off
  ere he win to the Tongue of Jagai.
But if he be past the Tongue of Jagai, right swiftly turn ye then,
For the length and the breadth of that grisly plain
  is sown with Kamal's men.
There is rock to the left, and rock to the right, and low lean thorn between,
And ye may hear a breech-bolt snick where never a man is seen."
The Colonel's son has taken horse, and a raw rough dun was he,
With the mouth of a bell and the heart of Hell
  and the head of a gallows-tree.
The Colonel's son to the Fort has won, they bid him stay to eat—
Who rides at the tail of a Border thief, he sits not long at his meat.
He's up and away from Fort Bukloh as fast as he can fly,
Till he was aware of his father's mare in the gut of the Tongue of Jagai,
Till he was aware of his father's mare with Kamal upon her back,
And when he could spy the white of her eye, he made the pistol crack.
He has fired once, he has fired twice, but the whistling ball went wide.
"Ye shoot like a soldier," Kamal said. "Show now if ye can ride!"
It's up and over the Tongue of Jagai, as blown dust-devils go,
The dun he fled like a stag of ten, but the mare like a barren doe.
The dun he leaned against the bit and slugged his head above,

But the redmare played with the snaffle-bars,
    as a maiden plays with a glove.
There was rock to the left and rock to the right,
    and low lean thorn between,
And thrice he heard a breech-bolt snick tho' never a man was seen.
They have ridden the low moon out of the sky,
    their hoofs drum up the dawn,
The dun he went like a wounded bull,
    but the mare like a new-roused fawn.
The dun he fell at a water-course—in a woeful heap fell he,
And Kamal has turned the red mare back, and pulled the rider free.
He has knocked the pistol out his hand—
    small room was there to strive,
"'Twas only by favour of mine," quoth he, "ye rode so long alive.
There was not a rock for twenty mile, there was not a clump of tree,
But covered a man of my own men with his rifle cocked on his knee.
If I had raised my bridle-hand, as I have held it low,
The little jackals that flee so fast were feasting all in a row.
If I had bowed my head on my breast, as I have held it high,
The kite that whistles above us now were gorged till she could not fly."
Lightly answered the Colonel's son: "Do good to bird and beast,
But count who come for the broken meats before thou makest a feast.
If there should follow a thousand swords to carry my bones away,
Belike the price of a jackal's meal were more than a thief could pay.
They will feed their horse on the standing crop,
    their men on the garnered grain.
The thatch of the byres will serve their fires when all the cattle are slain.
But if thou thinkest the price be fair,—thy brethren wait to sup.
The hound is kin to the jackal-spawn,—howl, dog, and call them up!
And if thou thinkest the price be high, in steer and gear and stack,
Give me my father's mare again, and I'll fight my own way back!"
Kamal has gripped him by the hand and set him upon his feet.
"No talk shall be of dogs," said he, "when wolf and grey wolf meet.
May I eat dirt if thou hast hurt of me in deed or breath,
What dam of lances brought thee forth to jest at the dawn with Death?"
Lightly answered the Colonel's son: "I hold by the blood of my clan:
Take up the mare for my father's gift—by God, she has carried a man!"
The red mare ran to the Colonel's son, and nuzzled against his breast;
"We be two strong men," said Kamal then,
    "But she loveth the younger best.
So she shall go with a lifter's dower, my turquoise-studded rein.
My 'broidered saddle and saddle-cloth, and silver stirrups twain."

The Colonel's son a pistol drew, and held it muzzle-end.
"Ye have taken the one from a foe," said he.
  "Will ye take the mate from a friend?"
"A gift for a gift," said Kamal straight; "a limb for the risk of a limb.
Thy father has sent his son to me, I'll send my son to him!"
With that he whistled his only son,
    that dropped from a mountain-crest—
He trod the ling like a buck in spring, and he looked like a lance in rest.
"Now here is thy master," Kamal said, "who leads a troop of the Guides,
And thou must ride at his left side as shield on shoulder rides.
Till Death or I cut loose the tie, at camp and board and bed,
Thy life is his—thy fate it is to guard him with thy head.
So, thou must eat the White Queen's meat, and all her foes are thine,
And thou must harry thy father's hold for the peace of the Border-line.
And thou must make a trooper tough and hack thy way to power—
Belike they will raise thee to Ressaldar
    when I am hanged in Peshawur!"

They have looked each other between the eyes,
    and there they found no fault.
They have taken the Oath of the Brother-in-Blood
    on leavened bread and salt:
They have taken the Oath of the Brother-in-Blood
    on fire and fresh-cut-sod,
On the hilt and the haft of the Khyber knife,
    and the Wondrous Names of God.
The Colonel's son he rides the mare and Kamal's boy the dun,
And two have come back to Fort Bukloh where there went forth but one.
And when they drew to the Quarter-Guard,
    full twenty swords flew clear—
There was not a man but carried his feud
    with the blood of the mountaineer.
"Ha' done! ha' done!" said the Colonel's son.
  "Put up the steel at your sides!
Last night ye had struck at a Border thief—
    to-night 'tis a man of the Guides!"

Oh, East is East, and West is West, and never the twain shall meet,
Till Earth and Sky stand presently at God's great Judgment Seat;
But there is neither East nor West, Border, nor Breed, nor Birth,
When two strong men stand face to face,
    though they come from the ends of the earth!

The Oracles

A. E. HOUSMAN

'Tis mute, the word they went to hear on high Dodona mountain
When winds were in the oakenshaws and all the cauldrons tolled,
And mute's the midland navel-stone beside the singing fountain,
And echoes list to silence now where gods told lies of old.

I took my question to the shrine that has not ceased from speaking,
The heart within, that tells the truth and tells it twice as plain;
And from the cave of oracles I heard the priestess shrieking
That she and I should surely die and never live again.

Oh priestess, what you cry is clear, and sound good sense I think it;
But let the screaming echoes rest, and froth your mouth no more.
'Tis true there's better boose than brine, but he that drowns must drink it:
And oh, my lass, the news is news that men have heard before.

The King with half the East at heel is marched from lands of morning;
Their fighters drink the rivers up, their shafts benight the air.
And he that stands will die for nought, and home there's no returning.
The Spartans on the sea-wet rock sat down and combed their hair.

INDEX

Titles are set in Roman, first lines in Italic, authors in capitals.

821.04 Me
Meyer
Breathes there a man: heroic
ballads & poems of the
English-speaking peoples.